New Adam

"Few books speak so boldly. John Bishop confronts the serious questions about masculinity and its counterfeits with biblical insight and theological depth. Rooted in Scripture and Tradition, illuminated by lived experience, he paints a vivid picture of authentic masculinity. I recommend *New Adam* to men of every age and vocation — from husbands and fathers to singles and celibates."

— **Dr. Scott Hahn**, Father Michael Scanlan, TOR, Chair of Biblical Theology and the New Evangelization at Franciscan University of Steubenville

"John Bishop is an outstanding teacher who is in tune with the aspirations and struggles of Christian men today. In this book, men searching for direction will find inspiration and wise guidance to help them navigate the challenges and uncertainties of modern living as they strive to become the men God made them to be."

— **Dr. Edward Sri**, theologian and senior vice president of Apostolic Outreach at FOCUS

"From mass shootings to collapsing performance in school and work, it's plain that our boys and men are in crisis — adrift in a culture with no guideposts for manhood. Until now, no one has shown a way out of the male malaise. At last, John Bishop's *New Adam* offers men a bold road map for forging a strong, biblically rooted masculine life. Essential reading for men and the leaders who guide them."

— **Brad Wilcox, Ph.D.**, University of Virginia Sociology Distinguished Professor

"This book is masterly. Although it explores ground already explored by others, no book I have read possesses the same power of empathy, the same fire of understanding. Franz Kafka says somewhere that we need to read books that 'wake us up like a blow to the head … a book must be the axe for the frozen sea within us.' John Bishop's *New Adam* is, without question, one of those rare, dangerous books."

— **Fr. Paul Murray, OP, Ph.D.**, Angelicum professor, author

"*New Adam* is an extremely important gift to the world and to the Church! Combining poignant stories, relevant data, and deep spiritual insights, Dr. John Bishop expertly unpacks the essence of true masculinity without falling into stereotypes or trite generalizations. Bishop clearly lives what he writes, and his personal experience infuses his book with a relatability, credibility, and insightfulness that challenges and inspires you to the core. A must-read for any guy serious about becoming or living as a true man … and there's plenty of heart and helpful perspectives to help women understand the men in their lives. I'm personally grateful Bishop didn't just personally form men in his sphere of influence, but wrote a deeply thought-provoking book to help all of us."

— **Pete Burak**, Renewal Ministries, V.P.

"The fruit of years of research and extensive field-testing in ministry to men, this powerful book offers Christian men a way forward out of cultural and personal malaise. Simply put, men are called to more. More than what the culture tells them they are or can be. More than the sin that ensnares them. This book offers a vision of Christian masculinity that is both powerful and practical. Full of stories, examples, and action steps, this book will inspire and direct men to conform themselves more closely to the *New Adam*. Highly recommended."

— **Dr. John Grabowski**, Professor of Moral Theology at The Catholic University of America

"New Adam is a clarion call for men at a critical turning point in history. For decades, gender wars have battered the identity of men and women, leaving many wounded and disoriented. Bishop's book becomes a compass — guiding men willing to face their wounds toward hope, healing, and the vitality of authentic manhood. This is not self-help but self-discovery. *New Adam* confronts the myth of 'toxic masculinity' head-on, offering instead a concrete theology of manhood that is both accessible and compelling. At its core lies one reality: Redemption of masculinity is found in relationship with God the Father. In the light of sin and the wounds it inflicts, Bishop calls men to the healing grace of the Cross and to embrace the vocation of being a man. This book raises men up through truth to rediscover the joy of their created identity."

— **Dr. Joseph Atkinson**, president emeritus - Catholic Biblical Association, JPII Institute professor

"In a time where there is so much confusion about what it means to be a man, husband, and father, John Bishop provides a clear blueprint for men of every age to become who they were born to be. Inspiring, spiritually rich, and practical, *New Adam* is not just a book for my own personal edification, but also for my sons and all the men I am proud to serve in my ministry as an evangelist."

— **Paul J. Kim**, speaker and musician

New Adam

GOD'S PLAN FOR MEN

John Bishop, Ph.D.

Our Sunday Visitor
Huntington, Indiana

Nihil Obstat
Msgr. Michael Heintz, Ph.D.
Censor Librorum

Imprimatur
Kevin C. Rhoades
Bishop of Fort Wayne-South Bend
October 27, 2025

The *Nihil Obstat* and *Imprimatur* are official declarations that a book is free from doctrinal or moral error. It is not implied that those who have granted the *Nihil Obstat* and *Imprimatur* agree with the contents, opinions, or statements expressed.

Scripture texts in this work are taken from the *New Revised Standard Version Bible*: Catholic Edition, copyright © 1989, 1993 National Council of the Churches of Christ in the United States of America. Used by permission. All rights reserved worldwide.

Excerpts from the English translation of the *Catechism of the Catholic Church* for use in the United States of America Copyright © 1994, United States Catholic Conference, Inc.—Libreria Editrice Vaticana. Used with Permission. English translation of the *Catechism of the Catholic Church*: Modifications from the Editio Typica copyright © 1997, United States Conference of Catholic Bishops—Libreria Editrice Vaticana.

Every reasonable effort has been made to determine copyright holders of excerpted materials and to secure permissions as needed. If any copyrighted materials have been inadvertently used in this work without proper credit being given in one form or another, please notify Our Sunday Visitor in writing so that future printings of this work may be corrected accordingly.

Copyright © 2026 by John Bishop
31 30 29 28 27 26   1 2 3 4 5 6 7 8 9

All rights reserved. With the exception of short excerpts for critical reviews, no part of this work may be reproduced or transmitted in any form or by any means whatsoever without permission from the publisher. For more information, visit: www.osv.com/permissions.

Our Sunday Visitor Publishing Division
Our Sunday Visitor, Inc.
200 Noll Plaza
Huntington, IN 46750
www.osv.com
1-800-348-2440

ISBN: 978-1-63966-395-8 (Inventory No. T3017)
1. RELIGION—Christian Living—Men's Interests.
2. RELIGION—Christian Living—Social Issues.
3. RELIGION—Christianity—Catholic—General.

eISBN: 978-1-63966-396-5
LCCN: 2026932521

Cover design: Karlie Brown
Interior design: Amanda Falk
Cover art: Karlie Brown

PRINTED IN THE UNITED STATES OF AMERICA

Contents

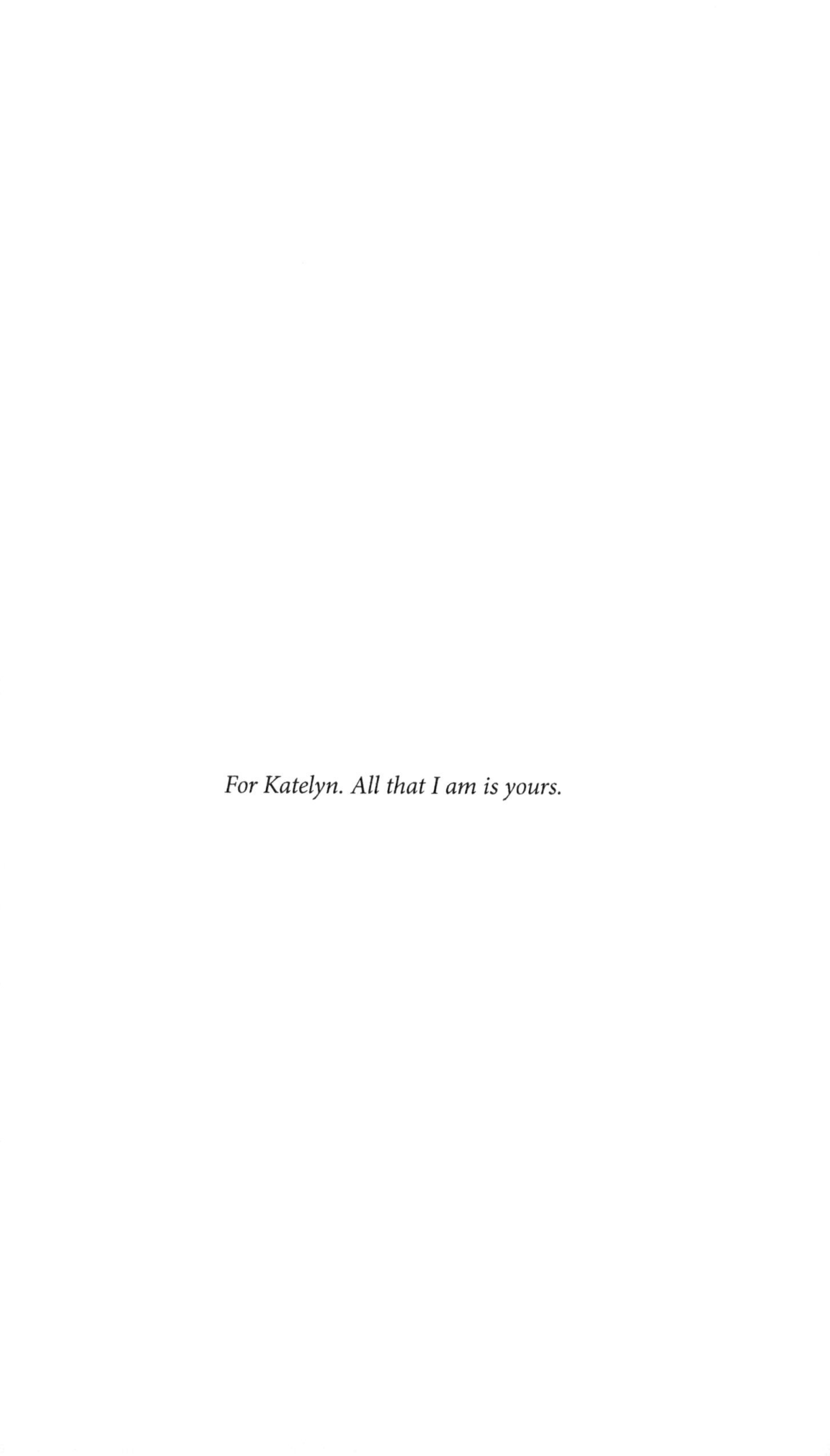

For Katelyn. All that I am is yours.

CHAPTER 1

Men Without a Map

Land diving is a ritual performed by the men of Pentecost Island, Vanuatu, in the South Pacific. The ritual begins on a bamboo tower, some sixty to ninety feet high. Fixed atop the tower are two vines approximately six feet shorter than the tower's height. Divers tie the vines to their ankles, build up their courage, and jump. The object of any diver is to leap headfirst as close to the earth as possible without touching it. Just to put that into perspective, divers hurtle through the air past six stories, trusting nothing more than a couple of jungle vines to break their fall. According to Guinness World Records, the g-force experienced by divers at their lowest point is the strongest in the nonindustrialized world.

Ariki Atan grew up on Pentecost Island. At thirteen, his turn came. The night before, he lay awake — skin prickling in the crisp air, heart drumming with a restless beat. For days he had been apart, cut off from the noise of the village, as the elders required. He had put his affairs in order, knowing that the dive could claim him. Now he slept, if it could be called sleep, at the foot of the swaying bamboo tower. In his mind, the jumpers of his youth descended — men he had admired, men who had proven themselves in the fall. Here, the leap was more than a dare. It was a rite, a liturgy written in earth and air. Boys climbed the tower. Men came down.

The practice of rituals like land diving raises an obvious question: "Why?"

Why have billions of adolescent boys across time and place risked life and limb to show themselves as "manly"? The old saying tells us, "Boys will be boys," but this adage overlooks a deep-seated desire enmeshed in the psychology of young males: Boys do not want to remain boys. They want to be men — and not merely in their own eyes, but in the eyes of the world.

Chun "Michael" Deng grew up in Queens, New York. Deng decided to stay in New York City for school, enrolling at Baruch College, part of the City University of New York.

On the morning of December 8, 2013, as his first semester of freshman year ended, his mother, Mary Deng, got the unexpected call that her son had been rushed to a hospital with traumatic injuries.

The next day, Michael Deng was dead.

Three young men had brought Michael to the hospital. When asked what had happened, their stories were inconsistent, but later scrutiny revealed that Michael had been injured in a fraternity hazing ritual called "The Glass Ceiling." In the ritual, pledges, who are blindfolded and wearing thirty-pound backpacks, push through a line of fraternity brothers who swing punches at the new recruit. The blows begin light, but as pledges traverse from one side of the room to the other, the violence becomes more severe.

In eighteen-year-old Michael's case, the violence proved fatal. At one point he was struck so hard that he collapsed, unable to stand. A kick to the head left his speech slurred. Still, the ritual went on. Then came the final blow — delivered by Kenny Kwan. Michael crumpled to the floor, unconscious. Panic rippled through the room. His brothers dragged him inside, changed his clothes, and waited. An hour of hesitation passed before they finally drove forty-five minutes to the hospital. By then, Michael's body was beyond saving. He died within twenty-four hours.

Why?

Some may puzzle over what drove Michael and Ariki. Others won't be surprised at all: they were boys who wanted to be seen as men. This fundamental male urge is simple but relentless. Behind the boisterous curtain of most boyhood antics is a desperate desire for masculine recognition. Ariki looked to his community. Michael looked to his fraternity. Both were willing to risk the extreme to claim their place.

Land diving and "The Glass Ceiling" are modern-day instances of initiation rites. The purpose of an initiation rite is to provide a bridge or a publicly recognized program through which one might travel from boyhood to manhood. Sometimes comical and regularly brutal, initiation rites have been a part of the male experience seemingly as long as there have been males. Though the modes vary, sociologists agree that the presence of male initiation rites is a near-universal phenomenon across time and place.[1] The Sambia tribe in Papua New Guinea mandates bloodletting. The Hamar tribe in Ethiopia requires young men to jump across a herd of cows. And natives in the Amazon River Basin require their boys to wear gloves packed with bullet ants. From the war paint of the South Pacific to the polo shirts of the United States, initiation rites are a mainstay of the male experience. The sheer lunacy of many initiation rites stands as a testament to the intensity of a boy's longing for manhood. Held within the mind's eye of every wild-eyed young boy is a picture, not of who he is, but of the man he wants to become. The trick to ensure that boys become good men is to make sure that they have the right picture in mind, then illuminate the path to achieve that picture.

What happens when a boy receives a distorted picture or is set on a crooked path? You get Michael Deng. You get millions wandering in a fog. Blur the picture, break the path, and boys are left to cobble together manhood on their own. In their insecurity, they wound themselves, their loved ones, their world. Want to help today's boys? Paint them a good picture. Cut them a path worth running.

Historically, most initiation rites aimed to instill in young men a set of praiseworthy masculine qualities. Many demanded some form of self-sacrifice, impressing upon boys the fact that self-gift is fundamental to mature manhood. Others, like those of the Pentecost Islanders, cultivated the courage to take risks. Nearly all required hard and unrelenting labor, teaching the value of work. In recent decades, there has been an explosion of literature on the importance of male rites of passage. These books matter — they chart a path into manhood. This book, however, is not one of them. It is less about a path and more about a picture, or about the fundamental images that form masculine self-understanding.

This book is driven by a single, central question: *What is the picture on which we should model our masculinity?* That picture matters: to the man striving to grow, to the father raising sons, and to the grandfather battling for generations yet to come. Without it, a man may set out on a journey without ever knowing his destination.

Whether we acknowledge it or not, most boys grow up with a specific picture of masculinity in their minds. It's not fully formed, but it's there — etched early and reinforced over time. A young boy might dream of driving a truck, wielding a jackhammer, or becoming the world's strongest man. An older boy might fantasize about wealth and the power to do whatever he pleases. A teenager might equate masculinity with sexual conquest, partying, and unchecked freedom. These images are often caricatures, but they are compelling. And unless someone intervenes — unless a boy is initiated into a fuller, truer vision of manhood — he may spend his life chasing a childhood fantasy.

That's why every society has a vested interest in forming a healthy sense of masculinity in its young men. Ours, instead, has done the opposite. Reacting to the sins of past men, we haven't reformed masculinity — we've crucified it. We've declared it toxic and called for its execution. But without a picture of manhood worth striving toward, we have no rites of passage worth walking through. And without those rites, men wander. Drunk on freedom but starving for direction, they leave behind them a wake of pain — borne not only by themselves, but by the women and children who suffer the fallout.

Yes, contemporary society has largely discarded the traditional picture of masculinity. But to be clear, this book does **not** argue for simply bringing that picture back unchanged. The old picture had its flaws — every picture does. Both Ariki and Michael grew up with a picture of manhood etched into their minds. For Ariki, it may have been a tribal leader; for Michael, perhaps a corporate executive. All pictures of masculinity are incomplete, but some are certainly better than others.

The old picture is gone. The modern one is broken. It's time to paint again. Not from nostalgia, but from the enduring, ancient truths about men. Whether they know it or not, today's males crave a renewed picture. This book seeks to offer one. Like every human attempt to portray divine creation, the picture in these pages will fall short. Yet we simply must try because the cultural alternative is so poisonous.

Stated concisely, the primary aim of this book is to paint a picture of true masculinity; that is, to paint a picture of genuine male flourishing. At this time in history, doing so is a perilous task. But the peril of the battle should be a reason for excitement. Saint Paul famously wrote that "where sin increased, grace abounded all the more" (Rom 5:20). God often allows evil to obtain a short-term victory so that good might more conclusively win the war. He allows lies to temporarily have the upper hand so that in the long run the truth might more vividly shine forth. Such is the case for men and masculinity. Our present culture has largely thrown masculinity out the window. On the one hand, that is a tragedy insofar as millions of men have been left without much-needed direction. On the other hand, it is an opportunity to paint a clear picture on a clean slate. Thus, for the Christian, the present crisis of masculinity should not be an occasion for panic, but rather for enthusiasm. After all, for Christians, men and women are indeed real things (not cultural fictions). "God created humankind in his own image … male and female he created them" (Gn 1:27). If men and women were created differently, it certainly makes sense that they would flourish differently. Authentic Christian masculinity is not a toxic concept deserving of alienation. On the contrary, it is a divine creation deserving of reverence.

Toxic Masculinity Is a Self-Fulfilling Prophecy

Sexuality scholar Asa Seresin uses the term *heterofatalism* to capture the state of modern relationships.[2] It refers to the widespread belief among women that relationally competent, marriageable men are in dangerously short supply. I saw hints of this in my own life. I was a single man who, neither in personality nor in physique, fit the Hollywood mold for any woman's "perfect man," but there always seemed to be a lot of women willing to go on dates. At the time, that was a great confidence boost! Over time, though, I began to recognize a pattern — one that had less to do with me and more to do with demographics. In Christian circles especially, the odds were heavily tilted in men's favor. At conferences, women filled the auditoriums. In graduate programs, the class rosters leaned female. At church, women outnumbered men almost everywhere. At first, I didn't think much of it. I chalked it up to divine favor.

Then everything changed. I convinced one of those women to marry me, and not long after, we had a daughter. When I entered my thirties, the imbalance that once seemed amusing began to feel bleak. I watched dozens of my friends — bright, faithful, beautiful women — walk through their thirties rarely, if ever, being asked on a single date. Many longed for marriage and children but found themselves waiting year after year for men who never came. I saw the pain in their eyes, sensed the quiet erosion of hope in their chests. Smiles gave way to silence. The light of expectation began to dim. They weren't dreaming of perfection — just praying that someone would show up. What had once felt like a personal blessing began to look like the outline of a dismal cultural collapse. I pray that when my daughter reaches adulthood, she will not inherit the same scarcity my peers were forced to endure.

I am alarmed by the state of modern masculinity, but today's man is not entirely to blame for today's man problem. I grew up in an age when most boys ingested, from an early age, a counterfeit picture of masculinity — not unlike the picture Michael Deng carried before his death. Though I personally was blessed with an exceptional father, many of my peers were not. Their fathers either looked the other way or actively encouraged a stunted caricature of manhood rooted in base, popular culture. That caricature of masculinity often involved a vocationally apathetic, sexually undisciplined jokester (like Billy Madison and Homer Simpson). And the fault is not only with fathers. Many mothers — reacting to the caricatures — smothered the masculinity of their sons. Many more left their sons suspicious of women by abandoning their marriages, as evidenced by the fact that roughly two-thirds of all divorces are initiated by wives.[3] The caricatures of the '90s and early 2000s then gave way to the largely reactionary YouTube manosphere of today. Baby boomer dads said, "Boys will be boys." The problem now is that their millennial and Gen Z sons are still boys ... just a couple of decades older. Their failure to launch is now a problem that could have been avoided had they been fed a different cultural picture.

After completing my master's degree, I spent eight years working on college campuses. Over those years, I witnessed hundreds of young men unwittingly buy into a version of masculinity that would leave them hollow for the rest of their lives. Consider your average secular college campus: a place filled with young people, cut off from the intergenerational structure of family life. In that environment, sex is seldom about union or family. Instead, it becomes a self-serving enterprise — stripped of consequence, commitment, or any expectation of permanence. The version of masculinity that thrives in that setting — marked by sexual license, endless entertainment, and low expectations — almost immediately begins to disappoint the men who embrace it. What feels like freedom at nineteen begins to feel like aimlessness at twenty-three, boredom by thirty, and despair by forty. The boys I knew as adolescents are now men in their thirties. The version of masculinity they learned as young men may have been helpful for navigating a frat party, but it left them ill-equipped to lead a family, form meaningful relationships, and build a life.[4] If you are one of those men, this book is for you. You can't control the picture you received. But you are accountable for the man you become.

If you take one thing from this book, let it be this: men need a new picture of masculinity, and it's worth fighting for. Why? Because men are in trouble. The last four decades have brought a crisis for men, as evidenced by nearly every relevant sociological metric, including a large and disproportionately male increase in suicide rates,[5] skyrocketing rates of fatherless children (9% to 25% since 1960 by *conservative* estimates),[6] and increasing rates of male incarceration (again disproportionate to that of females).[7] All of these statistics have risen alongside a corresponding plummet in male success in education.[8] Speaking particularly to my experience on college campuses, for many years now the college population of the United States has hovered right around 60% female and 40% male, meaning that for every three women who attend a college or university there are only two men. The deeper that I dug I found numerous studies chronicling the crisis. I spent time with authors like David Blankenhorn, Ray Baumeister,[9] Warren Farrell,[10] Leonard Sax, and most recently Richard Reeves.[11] Representing a diverse array of worldviews, all these authors agree that contemporary society has a serious man crisis.

What caused the crisis? Any full answer would require volumes. But here, I want to make a simple claim: our culture has confused men by stripping away their guiding principles. In labeling masculinity as universally toxic, we've set in motion a kind of self-fulfilling prophecy. Today's young men move through their formative years searching for direction, for some picture of what it means to be a man. Instead of guidance, our most influential cultural institutions meet them with an odd combination of scorn and license. The college campus, for example, condemns traditional masculine virtues with one hand while ushering young men into a sexual wonderland tailored to male appetites. It's a dangerous combination: pointed fingers and lowered standards.

And so, abandoned by the voices that should lead them, young men turn elsewhere, often to their peers, the internet, or the streets. There they absorb a counterfeit version of manhood: bravado without courage, appetite without self-mastery, self-centeredness rather than self-giving. Predictably, this counterfeit only deepens their dysfunction. Then, when the quality of men declines across society, that decline only furthers a negative perception. People become convinced that masculinity must be toxic by default. And so the downward spiral continues. In labeling masculinity as "toxic," our culture has unwittingly left young boys without a positive guide. Without such a guide, boys frequently become exactly the thing which the culture sought to destroy — toxic men. Toxic masculinity is a self-fulfilling prophecy.

What's the problem with killing masculinity? After all, it's easy enough to compile a laundry list of male sins. Men have started and carried out the bulk of wars and genocides. Most of history's great tyrants have been men. The lion's share of violent crimes is committed by men. For centuries, men denied women the right to vote, to own land, and to enter the most competitive professions. For millennia, most educational systems were tilted in favor of men. And of course, men are often promiscuous and sexually manipulative. Studies show that men are more likely to cheat on their spouses,[12] consume pornography,[13] and abandon their children.[14] By all counts, humanity has reason to be suspicious of men.

For these reasons, some within the contemporary psychological establishment argue that masculinity itself is a harmful invention that should be dismantled entirely. And curiously, one of the primary reasons given isn't just the damage that masculinity supposedly causes to women, but the toll that it takes on men themselves. A seminal voice in this movement is renowned psychologist Joseph Pleck. In his landmark 1981 book, *The Myth of Masculinity*, Pleck argues that the very concept of masculinity has a constricting, stress-inducing effect on men.[15] According to Pleck, when a man fails to meet the culturally imposed criteria for "being a man," he experiences shame, anxiety, and a persistent sense of inadequacy.

Pleck's core claim is simple: most men in American society — perhaps in all of Western culture — measure themselves against a fictitious ideal, one so narrow and exalted that almost no one can reasonably attain it. The result? Many men view themselves as "unworthy, incomplete, and inferior." Pleck and others point to cultural icons like John Wayne as symbols of post-World War II manhood. While such figures had traits worth admiring, Pleck argued that they also modeled a kind of *machismo*: a hyper-dominant, aggressive, and emotionally detached version of masculinity. This model, he claimed, was not only damaging to women, children, and society at large, but most of all to men themselves. Traditional masculine norms, in his view, saddle men with a lifelong burden of fear that they will never be enough. And for that reason, Pleck concluded, the concept of masculinity itself should be discarded.

While I ultimately disagree with Joseph Pleck's conclusion, I think he makes a powerful point. His critique speaks directly to my own experience, and it deserves special attention from today's Christians. I grew up in a strong Christian family, and, aside from an agnostic stretch during college, my faith has remained the central pursuit of my life. But my experience of twenty-first-century Christian churches is that, when it comes to masculinity, they tend to oscillate between two extremes. On one end of the spectrum are churches that have adopted a thoroughly "woke" mindset, in which gender difference is either ignored or outright denied. Unsurprisingly, these communities are often aging and shrinking. They offer a barely compelling vision of manhood and almost nothing that inspires young men to stick around. Their future is a graveyard.[16]

On the other end are churches that remain faithful to traditional Christian teaching, but frequently lapse into the very form of puffed-up, cookie-cutter masculinity that Pleck critiques.

Over the years, I've attended dozens of Christian conferences, many of which include a "men's session" and "women's session." The script is familiar. The men are ushered into an auditorium and greeted by a towering male figure — often an ex-athlete — who bellows a strange blend of Scripture and right-wing politics.

I'll never forget my freshman year of college, attending a conference with thousands of other students. When the room split for the men's session, we were met by a heavyset former football star screaming at the top of his lungs for us to "man up." Spit flew. His voice cracked. His face reddened. And I remember feeling vaguely embarrassed — was *this* what my faith had to say about being a man? And I was someone who played sports and loved the weight room. I could only imagine what my more artistically or intellectually inclined friends were thinking. The size of the speaker's biceps was only outmatched by the poverty of his vocabulary.

Sadly, this was not an isolated experience. The same caricature has repeated itself in retreats, churches, and men's conferences across the years. It's not manhood — it's cringy theater. It leaves far too many men feeling alienated, ashamed, and fed-up with what appears to be an emotionally stunted, cultlike sham.

So, Joseph Pleck had a point. And he is not alone in his appraisal.[17] In the midst of the 2018 #MeToo movement, the American Psychological Association (APA) published new guidelines that were meant to help mental health professionals treat boys and men.[18] These guidelines are the latest in a series of APA updates dating back to Pleck's work in the 1960s. Although the guidelines were not intended for the general public, they reinforced the country's impression of traditional masculinity by saying that "traditional masculinity — marked by stoicism, competitiveness, dominance, sexual license, and aggression — is, on the whole, harmful." For many in the APA, masculinity is an invention — literally a "construction" — of the cultural imagination. It is not a benign invention, but rather one that has caused widespread harm. Unrealistic standards of masculinity have not only harmed women and children; they have also produced widespread anxiety, depression, and even suicide for men. Thus, the "myth" of masculinity needs to be *deconstructed*. Traditional masculinity, this narrative says, is not only violent, oppressive, manipulative, and sexually rapacious, it is a stress-inducing poison whose garish qualities ought to be exposed and blotted out.

In an article published in the American Psychological Association's journal *Psychology of Men and Masculinities*, Brian P. Cole notes that the majority of research conducted on traditionally male psychological traits implicitly treats those traits as negative.[19] Cole asserts that in the 20-year history of that journal, perhaps the most globally influential psychological journal on masculinity, only 15% of the articles published took what he classified as a positive view of masculinity and the rest treated masculine traits as negative. Of course, negative opinions on masculinity are not limited to academia. In any given month, negative allusions abound in the entertainment industry (think, for example, of the bumbling/foolish television father perpetually outsmarted by his wife and adolescent children) and popular media. Both in academia and in society at large, masculinity has a bad reputation.

Modern culture's campaign to erase masculine identity has, by and large, succeeded. A favorable picture of masculinity has been predominantly erased. Why has this strategy been so devastatingly effective? Because it strikes at a uniquely male vulnerability. Compared to their female counterparts, there is often an insecurity for men concerning their own masculinity — something I will refer to as *masculine fragility*. Men tend to form their masculine identity through action, affirmation, role, and cultural script.[20] Men joke about being a "real man" or losing their "man card." Male banter often includes mocking the manhood of other men in a way that has no real parallel in female dialogue. In this way, the masculine sense of self can be fragile — not because men themselves are weak, but because masculine identity is, by nature, more easily challenged and more easily lost than its feminine counterpart. Masculine fragility makes men — especially young men — intensely driven to live up to their society's vision for manhood. Whatever that picture includes, they desperately want it.

If society wants its sons to become strong, present, intentional fathers, biology won't get them there. It takes a cultural picture of manhood. Biology may make a man a dad, but only culture can form him into a good father. And herein lies perhaps the most nauseating effect of the toxic masculinity movement. The rejection of masculinity is killing fatherhood. Today less than half of American children reach adulthood with both parents at home. And it's usually not dads who raise children in split families. Moms do. Approximately 80% of single-parent homes are led by mothers.[21] American fatherlessness has risen in lockstep with American contempt for masculinity. That's not accidental.

The deconstruction of masculinity has fueled the decline in fatherhood. Without a model to guide them, young boys become confused men. And confused men usually do not become fathers, at least not good fathers. By destroying masculinity, our culture has destroyed a boy's map to fatherhood. No masculinity, no fatherhood. And, to state the obvious, this is a painfully bad thing. As illustrated by groups like the National Fatherhood Initiative, the presence of an involved father positively correlates with a child's success in almost all relevant sociological metrics, including educational success, psychological stability, and future job performance. Conversely, the absence of an involved father does the opposite, correlating with things like poverty, infant mortality, and prison. To deconstruct masculinity is to deconstruct fatherhood, and to deconstruct fatherhood is to hurt children.

A Call for Renewed Masculinity

Contemporary men find themselves in crisis — and it's not a crisis entirely of their own making. Across nearly every sociological measure — marriage, fatherhood, education, mental health — men are in steep and steady decline. Rather than offering boys a noble picture to pursue, our culture has set itself to the task of erasing their path altogether. And given the inherent fragility of masculine identity, that erasure is particularly destructive. Instead of calling men to greatness, society has branded masculinity itself as toxic. But in doing so, it has created the very thing it condemns. Stripped of a healthy model, men have begun to imitate the broken caricature that they've been handed. The result is not less toxic masculinity, but more. The ideological assault hasn't purified masculinity — it has poisoned it.

So where do we go from here? In the face of "toxic masculinity," men seemingly find themselves with a choice. They must either (a) choose to live according to a toxic, machismo masculinity or (b) admit that masculinity is a myth and has no bearing on one's life. Pick your poison: machismo or myth. These are the only options available … or so the cultural narrative would have us believe. But are these all the options? Must masculinity be either machismo or myth? Is there a third choice?

Young men have begun to feel there must be. In fact, in the two years leading up to this book's publication, we have seen small but notable shifts in the data. Church membership has long been declining in the United States, yet the picture is changing among Gen Z. For the first time in several generations, young men are — at least in American demographics — more religious than women. According to a 2024 survey, only 34% of Gen Z men now identify as religiously unaffiliated, compared with nearly 40% of Gen Z women.[22]

This generational shift, though too recent to allow for sweeping conclusions, may indicate to us that young men are dissatisfied with the options presented to them and are looking to the Church to provide them a vision for their masculinity. There is reason to hope that we may be standing at the threshold of a masculine revival, one that could begin in the pews, spill into the streets, and echo through the culture.

If there is a route for such a masculine revival, it lies in neither machismo nor myth. Rather, it begins with a deeper appreciation for what might be called authentic masculinity — a vision that contemplates the God-given charisms of men and asks how those talents, dispositions, and strengths might be harnessed for the kingdom of God. The chapters that follow will celebrate sexual difference. It baffles me that in a culture as openly sexual as the United States, we are at the same time preoccupied with explaining away the differences between men and women. Why not celebrate those differences? Why not savor what the Creator has made?

This positive, difference-celebrating vision carries forward a project begun by the twentieth-century philosopher Karol Wojtyla, who would become Pope St. John Paul II. I spent many years as a student of Wojtyla, and I owe him an incalculable debt of gratitude. Wojtyla developed the notion of the unique charisms of women, which he termed "the feminine genius," placing it within a marital theology exalted by many for its beauty. This theology has provided a context for a greater reverential attitude toward women and femininity, but it has not yet proven as helpful in cultivating the same reverence toward men and masculinity.

Nevertheless, in these new times, humanity is facing new problems. One of those problems is the very real crisis of men, which threatens the life of society and the Church. Part of this problem's origin is the lack of a meaningful picture of what it is to be a man, the kind of picture to which young boys can aspire and thrive in as a result. All this is to say, our current times are in desperate need of a renewed theology of masculinity, or what might be termed the "masculine genius." Now, to be clear, men and women are equal in dignity and complementary in gifting. The nuanced yet profoundly complementary dimensions of men and women should be brought to the fore and celebrated.

So how do we begin to paint a picture of real manhood? Are there any clues to guide us? Thankfully, the road toward authentic masculinity didn't begin yesterday. Generations of men have walked it before us, and they've left behind markers for the journey ahead. The first is more of a warning than a recommendation: whatever vision we adopt, it cannot be so narrow that it excludes the full range of masculine expression. We don't need cookie-cutter masculinity. A man may be an athlete, or an artist, a professor, a farmer, or a father of ten. Our picture must be broad enough to embrace men of different temperaments, talents, and vocations. That's why the examples you'll encounter in the pages ahead span a wide range of personalities and callings. This point cannot be overstated. Next to erasing masculinity altogether — or denying the obvious reality of the sexual binary — the greatest danger is reducing manhood to a rigid, over-simplified counterfeit. That path doesn't form men; it suffocates them.

Second, any picture of manhood we draw must account for what I take to be the threefold reality of every human life: We are created, we are fallen, and we are redeemed. At its core, masculinity is good — full stop. God made man. Male strength, creativity, and courage are not defects to be overcome but gifts to be cultivated. And yet, man is free — and he fell. Under the weight of sin and a broken world, men are capable of grotesque, even monstrous things. But as Saint Augustine declared, "O happy fault!" — for even from the ruins, grace brings forth a glory that may never have bloomed in Eden. Any honest picture of masculinity must speak to all three truths: the goodness of man's origin, the darkness of his fall, and the splendor of his salvation. You'll find each of these explored in turn: creation in Chapter 2, fall in Chapter 3, and redemption in Chapter 4. The remaining chapters will apply the picture of masculinity to family life (Chapter 5), single life (Chapter 6), and the way forward for today's men (Chapter 7).

Finally, as Christians have always done, we should look to the heroes of our heritage. Christian tradition abounds with a wide array of masculine men. Poets, mystics, kings, politicians, preachers, martyrs, and businessmen all constitute concrete examples of masculinity. What does masculinity look like in the great men of our past? By rediscovering those ancient truths, we gain clarity to sketch a new picture for our time. No clearer picture will be presented to us of the vision God has for men than that of Adam, the first man, before the Fall.

CHAPTER 2

Man in Eden

At present, roughly 300 colleges and universities in the United States grant degrees in Women's Studies.[1] Degrees in Men's Studies? To my knowledge, there isn't a single one. The certification simply doesn't exist. For the record, I'm not convinced that either degree should exist. But the disparity reveals something important: For several decades now, both in academia and in the broader culture, our society has shown remarkably little interest in exploring the contours of the male human experience.

Amidst the absence of serious discussion about men in academia, the broader cultural conversation around sexuality has turned into a battlefield. For decades, some feminists have launched campaigns that most ordinary people find flatly absurd. From the bra-burning theatrics of the 1970s, to the "girl power" crusades of the 1990s, to the child sex surgeries of the 2020s, the feminist anthem seems increasingly deranged and out of tune. In response, an emerging "anti-feminist" counter-movement now charges in the opposite direction, firing its own salvos. Some figures push to extremes, even suggesting women should lose the right to vote. The media landscape has become a battlefield of over-simplified, left-vs-right artillery shells. Amid the blasts — like a classroom set down on the beaches of Normandy — today's boys are expected to learn manhood in a sexual war zone.

Given the fury of today's cultural maelstrom, it is increasingly important for men (and women) to step back from the fray. That was the instinct of Father James, the Dominican priest who prepared my wife and I for marriage. Katelyn and I had known Father James for years. When we asked him to witness our wedding, he gladly agreed — but with a few requests. One of them, the one that would shape me the most, was to spend a long weekend slowly reading through the entire wedding liturgy together — word by word.

And so we did. During that weekend, we didn't take personality inventories, sketch out mock budgets, or tally compatibility scores. Instead, we spent forty-eight hours in coffee shops, restaurants, and churches, walking line-by-line through the ancient text of the marriage liturgy. We would read a few sentences, pause, savor the words, pray, have another coffee, then move on to the next bit. The whole experience was as grounding as it was inspiring. From the exchange of vows to the blessing of rings, from the nuptial prayer to the final benediction, those ancient words gave us an ancient picture of marriage which guides our union even in the present day.

What struck me most in those days was how often Adam and Eve appeared in the liturgy. Again and again, the text returned to that first man and woman in Eden. And, I suppose, how could it be otherwise? When a man stands before his bride, preparing to give himself to her in covenantal love, who else should stand in the background but Adam? If marriage is a return to the beginning, then the beginning must be our guide.

I recall one point in the weekend when Father James made an observation about the liturgy, saying, "John, you'll notice that it is the man who makes his vows first in the marriage rite. There is a deep significance there. When you stand before Katelyn at the altar, you are Adam standing before Eve. Adam spoke first — "This at last is bone of my bones" (Gn 2:23) — and committed to her. Adam took the first risk, choosing Eve above everything else in the garden. In the security of his commitment, Eve was then free to respond in freedom to the first marriage request."

After speaking with Father James, I sensed that I was stepping into an ancient story of masculinity — one that began with Adam and still unfolds today. I looked to that first man not as a cultural controversy or a pawn in contested debates, but as a guiding picture, shedding light on truths about manhood that are both primal and urgently pressing.

This book will be of little use for shouting matches. It is not a weapon. It's a meditation, offered to those looking to reflect on the beauty of sexual difference. As you read it, I invite you to slow down. Step away — if only for a few chapters — from the din of battle. Step away from the sensational and the shrill, the caricatures and the slogans. Allow yourself to linger for a moment on truths too often overlooked, to sit quietly with realities too quickly stunted by today's sociopolitical combat. Let your imagination breathe again. Let your mind rediscover a subject flattened by controversy and drowned beneath the static of our age.

The Garden

What is the meaning of masculinity? What is the picture? On what model should we mold our lives? Well, Scripture gives us quite a few options, but the most foundational picture is the first one: Adam.

Scripture marks Adam's arrival with seven of the most profound words in all of divine revelation: "God created humankind in his own image" (Gn 1:27). There is no single truth about human nature more weighty than this. Humanity, endowed with a spiritual and immortal soul, is "the only creature on earth that God has willed for its own sake."[2] In his masterpiece of creation, God fashioned a capstone: mankind. And this capstone bears a likeness to its Creator.

This singular truth — what theologians call the *Imago Dei* — forms the most certain and enduring foundation for human dignity. We are created in the image and likeness of God.

Now the authors of Sacred Scripture could easily have stopped with those first seven words. But they didn't. The passage continues: "Male and female he created them" (Gn 1:27). That second line should go off like a bomb in our minds. We image God not only by virtue of what we share in common — our humanity — but also through our sexual differentiation.

God made males. God made females. And, as Pope St. John Paul II once said: "It is only through the duality of the 'masculine' and the 'feminine' that the 'human' finds full realization."[3] Both masculinity and femininity have something to teach us about God! Latent within the opening pages of Genesis is a profound claim: to become familiar with humanity as male is, in some real way, to become familiar with God. For this reason, discerning the contours of authentic masculinity, learning what it means to flourish as a man, is no small matter. It is a question with deep spiritual weight. It is theological.

Keeping this gravity in mind, let us begin our study of Adam's creation in the opening chapters of Genesis. Here, Scripture appears to lay out a hierarchical ordering of creation. God begins with the heavens and the earth before calling forth light. He separates the waters, forms dry land, and brings forth vegetation. He establishes day and night, then populates the skies with birds and the seas with fish. Next come the land animals: cattle, wild beasts, and crawling things. Finally, creation reaches its crescendo in the making of man.

There is a clear trajectory at play — a movement from lower, inanimate realities to higher, more complex life forms, culminating in the creation of humanity. God then gives dominion of all creation to the human race.

Everything we have said thus far takes place in the first chapter of Genesis. It is not until Chapter 2 that we are introduced to Adam and Eve by name. There, the sacred author records God placing Adam in a garden called Eden. The text reads as follows:

> The LORD God took the man and put him in the garden of Eden to till it and keep it. And the LORD God commanded the man, saying, "You may freely eat of every tree of the garden, but of the tree of the knowledge of good and evil you shall not eat, for in the day that you eat of it you shall die."
>
> Then the LORD God said, "It is not good that the man should be alone. I will make him a helper fit for him. So out of the ground the LORD God formed every beast of the field and every bird of the air, and brought them to the man to see what he would call them; and whatever the man called every living creature, that was its name." (Genesis 2:15–19)

Adam was placed in the garden alone, prior to the creation of Eve, which is confirmed by Saint Paul in 1 Timothy 2:13: "For Adam was formed first, then Eve."[4] Adam's solitude carries profound implications for his place within the created order. In the ancient account, when Adam first opens his eyes, he finds himself in a garden. This is an environment bursting with life and beauty: plants, animals, rivers, and sky. But one thing is missing. There are no other people. Just like any young man is alone before he marries, Adam is alone in the garden.

His first encounter with reality unfolds in a world populated entirely by what we might call "things": soil and stone, tree and stream, bird and beast, but no fellow human beings. This solitude reveals something essential about man: by nature, men seem more readily oriented toward things than toward persons. From the beginning, Adam's universe is composed of objects to observe, name, and tend — and so his perceptual habits are shaped accordingly. He is primed to engage with the world through work, discovery, and dominion.

Renowned psychologist Simon Baron-Cohen observes that across cultures, women tend to score higher in empathy — the ability to identify with and respond to the emotions of others — while men consistently score higher in systemizing, the drive to analyze, categorize, and construct rule-based frameworks.[5] Dr. Gregory Bottaro highlights this point, saying that, "By age five, the major cognitive difference between a boy's brain and a girl's brain is the ability to mentally rotate and manipulate objects."[6] On average, men tend to readily and naturally express this kind of capacity, though it is present in both sexes.

When describing a man's thing-centered disposition, I often use the word *externality*; that is, a general focus on objective achievement and fascination with the inanimate objects of creation. In everyday terms, masculine externality appears in the instinct to act: to move, to accomplish, to slip into "fix-it mode." Of course, this instinct has both positive and negative manifestations, but here we will focus on the positive. Male externality is a gift to the human race, to nations, to families, and to marriages. It has blessed humanity with philosophical and scientific systems. It has shaped the political structures in which civilizations flourish. It has built the homes in which families find shelter. It has served marriages, especially in moments when emotional distance helps for clear decision-making.

Arising out of Adam's externality comes a love, and indeed a sacred responsibility, to work the garden. Remember, before God formed Adam, Eden was barren — no shrub nor plant had yet sprung from the earth (see Gn 2:5). Then God placed Adam in the garden "to till it and keep it" (Gn 2:15). Without Adam's care, the garden would fall into disrepair. Adam's labor is not incidental; it is essential to the fulfillment of God's creative design. In this way, Adam doesn't merely do maintenance on the garden — he furthers God's creative act. And Adam's work continues to this day. Every time a man brings his intellect and will to bear on the world — every time he shapes, orders, builds, or cultivates — he participates in the creative action of God. Labor is no trivial matter. Indeed, work is a sacred thing.

What does this look like in practice? It looks like a contractor framing an office. An accountant building a spreadsheet. A software engineer writing code. An author crafting a sentence. Naturally, we're not speaking here of sinful activity — sin runs against the grain of creation. If the universe is a finely tuned engine, sin is the wrench that seizes its gears. In every noble profession, Adam's sacred mission is renewed. Like an automobile humming down the freeway, God's creative brilliance continues its course, carried forward through human hands across time and space.

These early passages of Scripture reveal something profound about the dignity of human labor: The *Imago Dei* shapes not only who we are, but what we do. It speaks not just to human nature, but to human activity. This truth applies, of course, to the work of both men and women. As we'll explore later, certain characteristically feminine forms of labor complement Adam's work in the garden. Nevertheless, it is significant that the first scriptural image of human work is Adam's work, which by its very nature was rooted in his mastery of the garden.

The Rite

The Babylonian creation story begins in blood. According to the *Enuma Elish*, the god Marduk rose to power by confronting the primordial goddess Tiamat. An ancient tablet records his grim resolve: "I will confront Tiamat and calm her rage. I will plunge into her and shatter her entrails. I will establish my rule and let it stand forever." Marduk does exactly that. He slaughters Tiamat, splits her corpse in two, and fashions the heavens and the earth from her mangled remains. But his bloodlust is not yet satisfied. Turning next to Kingu — another god — Marduk kills again. From Kingu's spilled blood, he forms mankind. Of this act, the text records Marduk saying, "Blood I will mass and cause bones to be. I will establish a savage — 'man' shall be his name. He shall be charged with the service of the gods, that they might be at ease."[7] If you were a young boy growing up in Babylon, this was your origin story. This was your model of the divine, your explanation of your purpose: to serve the gods, to be savage and enslaved. For decades, during the long dark years of the Babylonian exile, the people of Israel lived beneath the shadow of this picture.

Israelite fathers told their sons a different story. In so doing, they painted a very different picture of manhood. They spoke of Adam — not as the byproduct of war or the collateral of divine conflict, but as the deliberate handiwork of a good and sovereign Creator. That story gave young Jewish boys a picture of manhood rooted not in violence or utility, but in dignity and purpose. For Israel, creation was not born from a corpse. Man was not a slave to appetite. Imagine a father in exile 2,500 years ago, troubled by the lies his son is absorbing from Babylonian culture. So he pulls the boy aside and tells him a story — not of cosmic carnage, but of a garden. A man placed in it. A task given. A world to cultivate. Masculine icons rise and fall, and today's culture offers no shortage of contenders — some not too far from Marduk. But as for me, I want to model my life on the story that begins not as a horror film, but in a garden.

Jews and Christians have been meditating on the story of Adam for millennia, from the ancient Israelites to the Church Fathers, from medieval theologians to modern-day scholars and saints. One such meditation took place in Saint Peter's Square on October 10, 1979. Tens of thousands of pilgrims gathered beneath the Roman sky, eager to meet the newly elected Polish pope, John Paul II. Stepping into the brisk October air, he turned the world's attention not to politics or papal ceremony but to the garden of Genesis and the mystery of Adam. Before we consider what Pope St. John Paul II had to say, let us first return to the Scripture itself:

> Then the Lord God said, "It is not good that the man should be alone; I will make him a helper fit for him." So out of the ground the Lord God formed every beast of the field and every bird of the air, and brought them to the man to see what he would call them; and whatever the man called every living creature, that was its name. The man gave names to all cattle and to the birds of the air, and to every beast of the field; but for the man there was not found a helper fit for him." (Genesis 2:18–20)

Commenting on these passages, John Paul II says that Adam "finds himself from the very first moment of his existence before God in search of his own being, as it were; one could say, in search of his own definition … in search of his own 'identity.'" Adam is searching for what it means to be a person and what it means to be a man. He is looking for his place in the world, and the Lord is carefully leading him through a kind of rite of passage; that is, a journey of self-discovery.

What does Adam learn in this rite? Fundamentally, Adam

learns that he is a person. Adam rests in the knowledge that he is a son of the all-powerful, all-loving God! Adam knows that he is not the product of some cosmic accident. He is the pinnacle of the created order. And as a person, he stands over and above all creation as its steward.

How does Adam come to this realization? Scripture says that God forms "every beast of the field and every bird of the air" and brings them to the man to "see what he would call them" (Gn 2:19). And it is through this test that Adam gains the understanding that he cannot be equated with any other living species of the earth. Imagine the Lord presenting Adam with a fox, a deer, and a lion. Adam names each one, and in so naming he declares a dominion over them. Masters name servants and not vice-versa. For Adam, the act of naming becomes both an exercise of dominion and an act of self-differentiation: He comes to know himself more clearly by setting himself apart from the things he names. He sees that he is more than the plants, which possess no freedom, no intellect, no will. And the more he familiarizes himself with the animals, the more clearly he perceives that he is not ruled by base instinct or appetite. As he walks through this divinely-ordained rite of passage, Adam is becoming a king over the garden; that is, he gains facility as a ruler. He gains confidence that he exists on a plane over and above the animals. He is a person. He is a man, and as such, his instincts are made to bring the garden to life!

Throughout history and across cultures, the passage from boyhood to manhood has often been marked by a kind of test. Whether formal or informal, public or private, a man's rite of passage serves a crucial purpose: It channels the wild, risk-prone energy of a boy into the ordered and life-giving power of a man. This need for discipline and direction is not a social construct. It's far older than Babylon. The male disposition toward danger, competition, and recklessness is built into his very nature. Left unchecked, it becomes destructive. When properly channeled, it becomes strength. Any true rite of passage does for a boy what the Lord did for Adam: It impresses upon him that he is a son of the Father, the crown of creation, and entrusted with dominion over the garden.

Since the dawn of humanity, young men have carried an innate need for the channeling power of rites of passage. Their risk-prone impulses require direction rather than suppression, and such rites have long served as the decisive means of harnessing that restless energy. To understand why this is so, one illuminating guide is evolutionary biology, which traces the distinct roles men assumed within the herdlike dynamics of our earliest ancestors. The details of the evolutionary tree lend exquisite texture to the anthropology first revealed in Eden, offering natural confirmation of truths disclosed in revelation. Among the most striking of these patterns is a phenomenon which I will here refer to as *masculine expendability.*

Our faith teaches us that there was a first man, Adam, who was fully human and endowed with a soul. Science shows us that natural selection was the tool which God employed to bring humanity into existence. Among our hominoid ancestors, males played a more peripheral role in reproduction. Because a single male could impregnate multiple females, the reproductive system could afford to "lose" large numbers of males without threatening the survival of the species. Females, by contrast, were more biologically essential — necessary not only for conception but for gestation and care of the young. According to Ray Baumeister, in "many animal species, close to 90% of the females but only 20% of the males reproduce." The average male animal is "destined for reproductive oblivion."[8] Consequently, evolutionary pressures favored traits in males that lent themselves to risk-taking and high-stakes behavior: strength, aggression, competitiveness. In brief, men really are manufactured to be a bit wild. "Nature rolls the dice more aggressively with males than females, because it is easier to capitalize on wins and cut the losses."[9]

Modern science affirms what ancient wisdom long understood: men are wired for risk. Of course, none of this means that modern men are fated to behave like Neanderthals. But it does suggest that the evolutionary pressures which shaped the male genetic code can shed light on enduring features of male personality. Masculinity is, in many ways, a high-risk condition — something that must be achieved, and something that can be lost. That dynamic is not simply the result of biology; it is written into the logic of creation itself. As Genesis tells us, "God created humankind in his own image … male and female he created them" (1:27). In that divine image, masculine strength is not brute dominance. It is power brought under discipline — a force directed toward protection, provision, and sacrifice. The rite of passage is how a man learns to direct his strength.

The pattern in Genesis holds true today: a man's identity is forged in the crucible of adversity. There comes a time — there *should* come a time — when the wildness of boyhood is channeled into the strength of a gentleman. That discipline can happen anywhere: on a debate stage, a basketball court, or behind a musical instrument. Wherever it happens, the principle is the same — the exterior exercise channels the passion of a boy into the virtue of a man. The exercise of gaining facility over some arduous task impresses within the boy the knowledge he stands over and above creation as a human steward. Like Adam in the garden, a boy in a rite of passage gains both self-possession and self-knowledge. In modern terms, you might think of a coach or music instructor who not only (a) brings a young man to peak performance, he also (b) shows the boy their identity in the process. The athlete no longer obeys his base instincts, nor does he suppress them; in dominion, he directs them. The musician no longer wastes his brilliance, nor does he stifle it; in dominion, he puts his brilliance to work!

That is the shape of true manhood — neither emasculated nor debased. A mature man knows himself: who he is, and who he is not. Unlike the savage of the Babylonian gods, the picture given to us in Genesis is the picture of a gentleman.

Here I would be remiss if I did not speak directly to both single men and fathers. First, to the single men: At this point in your life, you are Adam alone in the garden. Live as he did. Learn to risk well by taking some smart ones. Learn to work the things of today's modern garden by devoting yourself to a profession. Do hard things that build virtue. Seek out experiences that reveal your true identity. When I worked with college students, I saw too many waste their single years — whether in the haze of parties or the glow of endless video games — forming habits that left them frustrated and unprepared for manhood. But I also saw others who lived differently. They built virtue, mastered professions, and deepened their identity as sons of God. Their adventures were not drunken weekends but pilgrimages and backpacking trips. They started businesses, ran marathons, and forged lasting friendships. They recognized their freedom and used it to cultivate the garden. They discovered who they were — and in doing so, prepared themselves for the rest of life. Do not waste your single years.

For the fathers. Show your sons the garden of this world. Be the dad who pours himself into adventures with them. Let them taste a wholesome wildness. When you see a spark in their work or studies, do everything you can to fan it into flame — open doors, build connections, clear the way. Teach your son to be a son of God by praying with him. And surround him with brothers — introduce him to other young men who are learning the same path to manhood. Adam's rite of passage was not a single event. God the Father journeyed through Eden with Adam. Do the same with your son.

The Woman

Before Eve's arrival, Adam's externality is on display. He is drawn to naming, to systematizing and ordering creation — to distinguishing one thing from another and assigning a proper place. Alongside this ordering impulse, Adam also carries a wild, risk-prone drive — a primal energy that serves him well as he works, explores, and cultivates the garden. This risk-welcoming, externally-focused wiring is not a flaw to be tamed but a gift to be channeled. It constitutes a kind of masculine charism — a distinctive strength that, when formed and directed, bears great fruit.

But something is wrong in paradise. Adam walks in harmony with nature, commands the beasts, and speaks face to face with God. He lives in a world without sin, without death, without need — and yet he aches. As the sacred author puts it, "The man gave names to all cattle, and to the birds of the air, and to every beast of the field; but for the man there was not found a helper fit for him" (Gn 2:20). Adam stands as steward over the whole created world, richer than any king, yet there is a hollowness in his joy. I think of men I knew during my years in Washington, D.C. — sharp, successful, surrounded by brilliance. Many were professionally accomplished … and perpetually single. They had the world by the tail, yet many of them carried a quiet angst they couldn't quite name. Adam's ache is something like that. What good is a kingdom, if no one is there to share it? "Paradise itself," writes St. John Chrysostom, "did not satisfy Adam … the company of angels was not enough; he needed a creature like himself."[10] So, what happens next? The text reads as follows:

> So the Lord God caused a deep sleep to fall upon the man, and while he slept took one of his ribs and closed up its place with flesh; and the rib which the Lord God had taken from the man he made into a woman and

> brought her to the man. Then the man said, "This at last is bone of my bones / and flesh of my flesh; / she shall be called Woman, / because she was taken out of Man." Therefore a man leaves his father and his mother and cleaves to his wife, and they become one flesh. And the man and his wife were both naked, and were not ashamed. (Genesis 2:21–25)

Imagine what that must have been like. Your entire existence has been spent working in a garden. Don't get me wrong — it's a beautiful garden. But at the end of the day, it's full of plants and animals. None of them see you. None of them speak your language. Then, out of nowhere, something appears — someone. And not just anyone: a woman. A gorgeous woman. And she's completely naked. And Adam rejoices! For the first time in Adam's life, his ache has an answer.

Eve may not have been created at the beginning, but she appears at the crescendo. The Genesis narrative follows a kind of ascent. Adam's journey begins with the naming of creatures — it ends in a cry of recognition. Just as God's creative order builds toward its crown, so too does Adam's speech rise to its highest and most intimate utterance: "This at last is bone of my bones / and flesh of my flesh" (Gn 2:23).

In that exclamation, Adam affirms Eve not as possession, but as equal. Not as object, but as other. He does not name her in the same way he named the animals; he receives her. She is not given to him as a tool, but rather she is revealed to him as a human mystery. Speaking to Adam's sacred encounter, John Chrysostom writes in the fourth century, "Behold a second self, a companion, a help like unto himself … fashioned not from the earth, but from his very substance, so that the bond between them would be closer, stronger, and more tender than any other."[11] Adam's long solitude — his silence among the trees, his dominion over the beasts — now has a higher purpose. It prepared him to see. His ache became a kind of training, a longing that refined his picture until he could finally recognize what he had never encountered before: a counterpart, made not above him or beneath him, but beside him. As Saint Augustine writes, "She was made not from the man's foot to be his slave, nor from his head to rule over him, but from his side — to be his beloved companion."[12]

The self-knowledge Adam gained before meeting Eve is now brought to bear in this moment of recognition. Because Adam knows that he is not an animal, he can look at Eve and proclaim, *"This is not an animal. She is like me. She is a person."* With that declaration, something deep within Adam comes alive. And as Scripture says, it is for this reason that "a man leaves his father and his mother and cleaves to his wife" (Gn 2:24). In other words, the encounter that happens here, between the first man and the first woman, is so profound as to immediately become the very center of Adam's existence. Everything in Eden and all other relationships must give way to the relationship that Adam now has with his woman, Eve.

While Adam's dominion over the things of the garden lies close to the core of his masculine identity, it is only here — standing before Eve — that the picture is complete. He is no longer merely the steward of Eden. He is now the guardian of Eve's identity. What he did outwardly, with the earth, was meaningful. But what he does now, in this encounter with Eve, is sacred. The work of his hands gives way to the work of his heart. The self-knowledge he gained in the garden until now came largely by contrast: *I am not like the plants, nor like the animals.* But here, for the first time, he learns through communion. Face to face with another who shares his very humanity, he exclaims: *I am the same as you. You are bone of my bones!*

In Adam, Scripture gives us the most foundational picture

of what it means to be masculine, and this is the picture of masculinity that we should pass along to our sons. What are Adam's essential attributes? Adam is a man who exists in dominion over his garden and in communion with Eve. Adam affirms Eve. By his actions, he shows Eve that she exists on a higher plane than anything else in the garden. Confident in himself, Adam affirms Eve in their common humanity and in her beauty as a woman. In his first words to her — "You are bone of my bones and flesh of my flesh" — he echoes what he learned in his solitude: *You too are more than dirt. You are more than the plants, more than the animals. You are woman. And I am yours.*

Here I want to speak to what I have come to regard in my own journey as a man, husband, and father as both the most difficult and the most essential task of manhood: to provide my wife with the physical, relational, and emotional space in which she feels safe, desired, and affirmed in her unique value as a human and as my woman. This is what Adam did for Eve. From the security of his own identity as son, Adam affirmed Eve as daughter and as bride. In all her feminine beauty, she reveled in his gaze. She rested in confidence that she stood at the very center of his garden. In his protection, she was utterly safe, not only physically but also emotionally. Adam's custody over himself and over his garden created a space where she, in her vulnerability, could entrust herself to him, and where their children could grow. Your job as a man is to become a new Adam.

This picture of manhood confronts us with a series of questions — questions that apply as much to single men in formation as to married men in family life. For Adam, everything in the garden — the plants, the rivers, the animals — was ordered toward the person of the garden: Eve. Creation served communion. The garden served the person.

So what about you? Do the things of your life — your work, your possessions, your ambitions — stand in service to the people of your life? Or have you flipped the order, making people serve your things? Are you the kind of man who can shelter a family physically, spiritually, and emotionally? Are you cultivating the skills to work the "garden" of today's economy? Are you praying and fasting so that your interior identity as son becomes ever more secure? Are you guarding your chastity so that your woman feels safe with you? Have you channeled your risk-prone spirit into the emotional and relational maturity of a gentleman?

Men are not machines. They do not live by output alone. Good men are not energized solely by the prospect of building a business or turning a profit — they come alive at the possibility of romance and new life. They know how to affirm their wives. They form deep friendships and allow themselves to be intimately known. And when it comes to children, yes, they provide and protect — but perhaps more importantly, they play. The father tossing his child in the air or crouching to meet a toddler eye-to-eye is not retreating from masculinity; he is fulfilling it. A good man exercises dominion over the things of his life, yet he bends every one of them to serve the people entrusted to his care.

Several years ago, I had the privilege of standing in the wedding party of a very good man, Jake. It's always a gift to linger behind the scenes and witness the more quiet and intimate moments of a wedding day. From the very start, all the guests had the same sense: this one was going to last. And it has.

The groom wasn't a saint. Everyone who knew him knew that he had his flaws. But he was steady. Hard-working with a low-level management job at a local corporation. He had begun to build something: a life, a profession. You might say he was good at tending his garden. And people respected him. Figuratively speaking, he was not only the kind of person who could tend a garden but also the kind who could protect it. But when that young man stood at the altar and saw his bride walking toward him, he nearly melted. Like Adam, his eyes rejoiced in what they saw. Everything that he had built or would ever build, he built for her.

My favorite moment took place later that night at the reception. I watched as a young boy approached the head table with his father and the pastor. The father crouched beside him, rested a hand on his shoulder, and pointed to the groom. "That could be you someday," he said. The boy looked on, wide-eyed. There was a brief pause. Then the pastor, wise and attentive, gently pointed across the room to a middle-aged dad spinning in circles with his giggling children. "Yes," he added, "and that could be you too." On that brisk November evening, a boy was given a picture of manhood. He saw a new Adam. I hope the boy never forgets it.

CHAPTER 3

Men in Sin

The Christian view of humanity can be summarized by saying that all people are capable of both breathtaking good and grotesque evil. Humans are often Godlike and frequently gross. Both qualities are on display in the life of King David, a man who I find eternally relatable. David was once a boy who slayed Goliath. He wrote psalms over 3,000 years ago that inspire conversions today. He led Israel into unprecedented wealth. By all accounts, he was a man among men: poet, warrior, king, lover … and a luxury-loving, cowardly, sex-obsessed murderer.

David's sin with Bathsheba is one of history's clearest and characteristic portraits of fallen masculinity. When his army went off to war, David stayed behind in Jerusalem, indulging in comfort rather than fulfilling his duty. From his palace rooftop he saw a beautiful woman, Bathsheba, bathing in the sun. He summoned her, slept with her, and she conceived. Ashamed, David scrambled to cover his sin. First, he tried to trick her husband

Uriah. When that failed, he sent Uriah to the front lines to be killed, essentially butchering a friend to cover an affair. Uriah's death opened the door for David to marry Bathsheba, and the cover-up was complete.

Every man is a bit like David. Shame in the interior life results in an emotionally distant, belligerent exterior life. Shame can spring from many places — lust, greed, inadequacy, embarrassment — but the pattern is always the same. And if you think this corruption lives only "out there" in the marketplace or the culture, you're deceiving yourself. The pattern lives inside every man's heart. I remember one evening when my toddler tugged at my arm, asking me to play. I sat slouched in a chair, scrolling through news feeds and social media, chasing the next dopamine hit while oblivious to the boy standing right in front of me. Nothing dramatic — just another long day, just another easy escape. He tugged at my arm again, and from the corner of my eye I caught my wife Katelyn watching. Ashamed, I turned away and brushed my son aside. In that small act I saw the truth: David's story is my story. My own male heart, which is capable of heroic self-gift, is also capable of cowardly self-absorption. Yours is too. We are made to be present and protective. Yet, ashamed, we hold ourselves at a distance. We dominate those weaker than we are. The pattern is ancient, but it persists.

Adam's Sin

What existed in David began with Adam. The first man had been given everything: a garden paradise and a gorgeous woman. But the harmony of Eden would not last. An ancient being, cunning and cold, slipped into the garden. The Scripture reads as follows:

> Now the serpent was more crafty than any other wild animal that the LORD God had made. He said to the woman, "Did God say, 'You shall not eat from any tree of

> the garden'?" The woman said to the serpent, "We may eat of the fruit of the trees of the garden; but God said, 'You shall not eat of the fruit of the tree that is in the middle of the garden, nor shall you touch it, or you shall die.'" But the serpent said to the woman, "You will not die; for God knows that when you eat of it your eyes will be opened, and you will be like God, knowing good and evil." So when the woman saw that the tree was good for food, and that it was a delight to the eyes, and that the tree was to be desired to make one wise, she took of its fruit and ate; and she also gave some to her husband, who was with her, and he ate. Then the eyes of both were opened, and they knew that they were naked; and they sewed fig leaves together and made loincloths for themselves.
>
> They heard the sound of the LORD God walking in the garden at the time of the evening breeze, and the man and his wife hid themselves from the presence of the LORD God among the trees of the garden. (Genesis 3:1–8)

Adam sinned. And this sin fundamentally altered his relationship with all of reality. When people today read this story, they often focus on what Adam did: he ate the "fruit of the tree." Relatively little is said about what Adam did NOT do. That is a noteworthy mistake, because from the earliest centuries of Christianity, Adam's silence was noted as his first sin. In the fourth century, St. Ambrose of Milan commented on the above passage, asking, "Why did Adam not ward off the serpent?"[1] In the same time period, St. Ephrem the Syrian says that it was not right that Eve should "confront the serpent alone."[2] Similarly, St. John Chrysostom, commenting on Adam's failure to protect Eve, says that it was fully within Adam's power to stop the serpent, but instead, "He kept silent and took the fruit."[3]

In Genesis 3, we are given a glimpse into a shame that strikes at the very heart of the masculine soul. After sinning, Adam hides. He withdraws not only from God but from Eve, cloaking himself behind trees and fig leaves. His shame renders him inactive. He cannot defend, cannot speak, cannot step forward. He shrinks in shame.

What is shame? Before their sin, Scripture tells us that Adam and Eve were naked yet "were not ashamed" (Gn 2:25). But after sin, shame entered the human story. Shame arises when our response to sin becomes distorted. For Adam, the clearest sign of this distortion is his lustful gaze. His look toward Eve is no longer one she can trust. He no longer protects her; instead, he grasps for her, seeking to use her as an object. Eve knows it. Her act of covering herself is a rejection of Adam's disordered gaze and, at the same time, an invitation to remember how he saw her before sin.[4] It's as if she were saying, "You won't see my body again until you learn how to see it as you once did."

While shame can serve a protective function, it can also corrode the soul. Contrast this destructive form of shame with a productive sense of the word guilt. Guilt over genuine wrongdoing can inspire change. Guilt says, "You did something wrong." Shame says, "You are something wrong." Guilt prompts repentance, confession, and reparation. Shame paralyzes. It confuses a man's identity with his failure. Guilt says, "You have sinned, now make it right." Shame whispers, "You are your sin. Hide."

This is precisely Adam's condition. "I was afraid, because I was naked; and I hid myself" (Gn 3:10). That phrase — "I was afraid" — reveals that this is a man who no longer feels safe in his own skin. His nakedness now feels sinful. Once at home in his body and at peace with his world, Adam now experiences alienation on all fronts. The garden, which once bent to his hand in joyful cooperation, now bristles with thorns. His body, once governed by reason and directed by love, now threatens to betray him. His passions, stirred by Eve's beauty, no longer serve the good. What was once integrated is now fractured — and Adam knows it.[5]

As is the case with so many men, Adam is fully aware of his twisted desires. He is fully aware of the monstrous things that he feels, and this awareness becomes an insecurity. From this insecurity flows a distinctively masculine shame. It is the fear that Eve and the world will glimpse the ugliness which he can scarcely admit to himself. It is a panic at the thought that someone else will find him out.

Just as the woman hides the parts of herself most susceptible to lust, so the man hides the parts most susceptible to embarrassment. After Adam eats the fruit, Genesis 3 records God's words: "Cursed is the ground because of you; / in toil you shall eat of it all the days of your life" (Gn 3:17). The word translated as "toil" is the Hebrew word *iṣābōn* (עִצָּבוֹן). The term conveys pain, sorrow, grief, and hardship. It indicates more than just hard work; it suggests labor marked by suffering, anxiety, and/or distress. Prior to the fall, Adam's work was a participation and extension in God's own creative action. After the fall, his labor becomes burdensome, marked by frustration and resistance. *Iṣabon* captures this shift: from joyful dominion to painful striving. Adam's relationship to his work has changed. At this point, we are in a position to understand Adam's shame before Eve.

Consider how Adam first presented himself to her before sin. Adam stood before Eve as the king of the garden. Figuratively speaking, he was the richest man to ever live, because the entire world existed under his stewardship. Everything around him obeyed his word. The ground yielded fruit. The animals bent to his voice. And when he saw Eve, he saw her as every woman longs to be seen: with wonder, with delight, with a gaze that says, *You are the one, the only one.* He beamed at her presence and surrendered his whole being in love.

But after sin, Adam is haunted by the knowledge that something has changed. He is no longer master of the garden. The soil that once yielded to him now resists. His labor is meager, fickle, and fraught with blunders. And when he looks at Eve, his mind is no longer whole. One part of him still delights in her, but the other part wants to use her. He knows it. And perhaps worse, he knows that *she* knows it. He is no longer the king, no longer the lover she met at the dawn of creation.

In the mire of today's world, countless men carry the weight of shame. It shows itself in the husband who feels he is failing at work, in the veteran haunted by the scars of war, or in the father who fears he has wounded his children. Yet perhaps nowhere does shame surface more powerfully than in the realm of lust — and no expression of lust is more pervasive than pornography.

In over a decade of working in collegiate and men's missions, I have had hundreds of conversations with men battling porn addiction. Many began compulsively viewing it immediately upon the onset of puberty. And they can hardly be blamed. After all, every boy with unrestricted internet access has, through a computer or smartphone, the equivalent of a porn shop in his bedroom. For them, the very lens through which they see sexuality has been shaped by a grotesque industry — one that, with a few clicks, hands boys (and girls) whatever twisted fantasies they can imagine. And without serious intervention, what begins as adolescent experimentation hardens into lifelong bondage.

What makes the present moment even darker is that pornography is only growing worse: more widespread, more intricately twisted to exploit desire. Artificial intelligence now produces digital "girlfriends," serving as easy companionship for lonely men in their hiding places. As the industry becomes more alluring, men's grasp on reality grows more fragile and they become enslaved to their appetites. I have just recently started speaking popularly on men and masculinity. In my talks, I often address pornography, and already on two occasions men have approached me with devastating stories related to child pornography. Once it was a father, just released from a four-year prison term. The second time it was a grandfather now raising his grandchildren after his stepson's imprisonment for the same vice. Few things have convinced me of the demonic more than the grotesque reach of the pornography industry.

Today's men are indeed just like Adam. So, what does today's man do? Like Adam, he hides. He turns his shame into a shield. He covers himself, withdraws behind guarded distance, and lapses into silence. The digital world only makes it easier to settle into that hiding place — almost as if Adam's fig leaves had been replaced by the glow of a smartphone. Adam's silence becomes the enduring template of fallen manhood — not only for him, but for you, for me, for every man who follows in his steps.

Dominance

When a man hides on the inside, something always happens on the outside. The concealment of his true self — his fear, his shame, his insecurity — never remains purely internal. It takes shape in his posture, his presence, and his interactions with others. And when it does, it tends to follow one of two paths. For some men, it hardens into dominance. They become the tough guy: brash and aggressive, callous toward other men and lustful toward women. For others, the hiding turns into distance. They become the quiet man: emotionally absent, unwilling to speak, the father who fails to protect his daughters or correct his sons. In both cases, the hiding continues. It's just wearing different clothes.

We'll look at each of these men in turn: first the dominant man, then — what is perhaps more common in today's world — the emotionally distant man.

After Adam's sin, the Lord speaks to Eve — and in doing so, delivers a sobering prophecy about the brokenness that will plague male-female relationships. "Your desire shall be for your husband," God says, "and he shall rule over you" (Gn 3:16). These words capture, with haunting clarity, the distorted dynamic that has marked human history since Eden. What was once a union of mutual self-gift is now strained by insecurity, fear, and perhaps most fundamentally, shame.

Dominance becomes Adam's defense. The man who once stood in awe of the woman now seeks to possess her. It is important to recognize that this dynamic is not part of God's original design. The impulse to dominate is not a feature of masculine identity, it is a deformation of it. Domination emerges not from the man who is confident in his strength, but from the man who is afraid he has none.

Many men know the type: a man feels small at work, unseen at home, or insecure in his relationships. Rather than face that shame, he puts on a mask of toughness — loud at the bar, quick to fight, needing to prove his strength. The brash exterior covers an interior insecurity.

The domination of women by men is not a side note in the story of sin — it is one of its central themes. In the case of the dominant husband, the very same man who should have laid down his life for his woman now seeks to control her. This is not strength. It is cowardice dressed in machismo clothes. When men dominate women — through violence, manipulation, or coercion — they commit a grave injustice against the very person God gave them to love and protect. In this way, dominance is a corruption of Adam's sacred role as the biblical head of the first family.[6] Dominance is a weak, shame-induced counterfeit of true headship.

While male domination is indeed nauseating, I would be remiss not to note a widespread misreading of authority in today's culture. Many have come to believe the lie that the only form of authority men can exercise — and are even biologically wired for — is its perversion: domination. This is simply false. Occasionally you run into people who slap the term "patriarchy" on almost any instance of strong male leadership. Such people do a disservice to humanity. Patriarchy in its authentic sense is not about self-exaltation but about self-gift: laying down one's life, protecting, and providing for one's family. The world needs more of that! When skeptics read the expression of male leadership as manipulation or covert control, such suspicion paralyzes men, leaving them hesitant and uncertain in the exercise of the very authority that they are called to practice.

A historical narrative is circulating which claims that gender relations in past societies were structured almost entirely to benefit men. There is no denying that women in history have often suffered from unjust limits and oppression. But it is difficult to accept the claim that civilization itself was little more than a male conspiracy.[7]

Consider a thought experiment: if an alien were to visit a European city in the 1500s, it would find men dying in wars, laboring in the most dangerous trades, and enduring hardships to bring food home and secure shelter for their families. If that same alien leapt forward in time to the present, it would again find men, particularly at the bottom rungs of the socioeconomic ladder, disproportionately imprisoned, executed, unemployed, and killed on the job. If our alien observer focused exclusively on these facts, he might reasonably conclude that human society had for centuries been structured to benefit women — shielding them from the worst fates and sacrificing men instead. Of course, that would be a false inference. But it is the same erroneous reasoning used by anyone who claims that men, in some universal sense, have always been out to oppress women.

The truth is that both extremes — the abuse of authority

through domination and the rejection of authority through suspicion — distort authentic manhood. Real patriarchs neither crush nor cower; they serve. But when a counterfeit patriarchy prevails, a vicious cycle begins. The radical feminist critic suspects all masculinity to be oppressive, and men shamefully retreat under the weight of this suspicion. Shame breeds insecurity, and insecurity lashes out in anger. The outburst then confirms the critic in her suspicions, and the cycle repeats itself like the self-fulfilling prophecy we talked about in our first chapter. Shame begets insecurity, insecurity begets distorted living, and distortion begets more shame. The only way out of this downward spiral is the recovery of a genuine, life-giving masculinity — a masculinity that stands firm in strength, serves without fear, and refuses to be paralyzed by the incessant critiques of a suspicious age.

Distance

Having worked full-time with men for several years, I have heard countless stories of masculine failure. And of all the sins that surface, the most common — and perhaps the most destructive — is the one that I call "masculine distance." At its core, this sin is the refusal to draw near. Like Adam in the garden, men retreat when they feel ashamed. I see it everywhere: in the absent father, the avoidant husband, the shallow friend. Few stories capture the devastation of this absence more starkly than that of my friend, Joshua Broome, and his father.

It was an April morning when I invited Joshua to speak to a group of men in my hometown of Des Moines, Iowa. I had never heard Joshua speak before, but a good friend had recommended him as a speaker, so I had reached out.

Joshua stepped out of the hanger at the Des Moines airport, slid into the passenger seat of my car, and headed off to lunch with me. He did an exceptional job as a speaker later that evening, sparking profound conversions in dozens of men.[8] But over the first couple of hours, I got to know the man behind the recommendation a bit more personally. By the end of our meal, I knew that I had met someone rare — someone with a singular perspective on the wounds that plague modern men.

At nineteen, Joshua moved to Los Angeles. Like many before him, he hoped to become an actor. To pay the bills, Joshua started working at a bar. One night, a group of attractive women struck up a conversation and asked him if he wanted a job as an actor — a porn actor. Curious and flattered, Joshua agreed to meet with an agent. When Joshua met with the agent, some of the first questions involved Joshua's family background: "Tell me about your family and where you come from." Those questions struck a nerve.[9]

Joshua Luke Broome had been born outside Charlotte, North Carolina, to a loving teenage mother. His father, however, had married another woman, raised a new family, and settled just a few miles away. Joshua grew up seeing his father around town, but never inside his home. His dad was always near, but never available. In other words, he was physically present, yet personally absent. Joshua recounts in his book: "The absence of my father in my life caused me to feel inadequate and somehow unworthy, and my high-achiever personality compounded the crisis as I tried to compensate for the feelings of poor self-worth. … I eventually started to act out in all the wrong ways."[10]

The absence of Joshua's father is often exactly what sin looks like in millions of men. And in his case, it had a devastating effect on the trajectory of his son's life.

In his interview with the agent, Joshua admitted that he was from a broken home — exactly what the agent wanted to hear. The first offer came soon after. Joshua accepted. Six years later, he had starred in nearly one thousand adult films. By 2012, the industry crowned him its top male performer. By their standards, he had made it.

Though both sexes struggle with relational intimacy, what I am calling "distance" seems to flow more frequently from men. Masculinity is designed to be outward-facing. That external focus, while positive in the many ways in which it allows men to protect and provide for others, also carries real danger. When disordered, it warps the masculine heart. Instead of being drawn toward people, men become absorbed in tasks, objects, and accomplishments. The male ego drifts from relationship and settles in the realm of performance. For the warped man, distance becomes a default. For this man, it is much easier to pour hours into a project than to speak to a spouse. It is easier to build a business than to build a bond with a son. In this way, the externality of men, left unchecked, becomes a hiding place, and then a prison — another tree in the garden behind which Adam conceals himself.

The psycho-emotional havoc unleashed when men hide will likely never be fully chronicled. Their absence creates spiritual and personal vacuums throughout society. I remember reading Meg Meeker's *Strong Fathers, Strong Daughters* as a young husband and father. When my wife was pregnant with our first — a girl — Meeker's opening lines stopped me in my tracks:

> After more than twenty years of listening to daughters — and doling out antibiotics, antidepressants, and stimulants to girls who have gone without a father's love — I know just how important fathers are. I have listened hour after hour to young girls describe how they vomit in junior high bathrooms to keep their weight down. I have listened to fourteen-year-old girls tell me they have to provide fellatio — which disgusts them - in order to keep their boyfriends. I've watched girls drop our varsity tennis teams, flunk out of school, and carve initials or

> tattoo cult figures into their bodies — all to see if their dads will notice.[11]

Meeker has one enduring message for dads: the *people* of your life need you, and they need you more than the *things* of your life need you. And of course they need the best of you. As Meeker continues, they need "every ounce of your masculine courage and wit … your strength, your courage, your intelligence, your fearlessness, your empathy, your assertiveness, and your self-confidence." At this point, the damage wrought by distant men — whether emotionally, physically, or both — is not a theory. It is a towering psychological fact. When Adam hides from the people in his garden, there is scarcely anything that can take his place. Indeed, when a man withdraws, the people who need him most feel the chill first. A son waits for a father's blessing — the steady voice that says, "You have what it takes." A daughter listens for the quiet assurance, "You are worth protecting." A wife strains to hear, "I see you, and I choose you." When those words go unsaid, wounds open. Families begin to orbit an empty center.

Research only confirms what broken hearts already know. Studies show that when men feel their masculinity threatened, they default to stoicism — enduring physical or emotional pain without a flicker of distress. Military data adds a sharper edge: Soldiers who question their own manhood report diminished closeness, connection, and openness with their partners. The more they overcompensate, the greater the gulf grows. Distance breeds more distance, a tragic feedback loop that leaves spouses isolated and children unsure where to look for strength.[12]

This, finally, is the cost of male absence. The masculine impulse toward the external, meant for brave protection and fruitful labor, becomes twisted into a mask that hides the very face it was made to reveal, and humanity suffers. The garden still needs a guardian; Eve still needs Adam's awe; children still wait for the Divine Father's echo in their earthly father's voice. Until men step out from behind the trees — until they close the gap between presence and performance — the world will continue to feel their lack.

Christ taught us to pray, "Our Father," not as metaphor, but as revelation. The earthly father is meant to be a living sign of the heavenly one. When that sign vanishes from our experience — when men retreat from the lives of their wives and children — it is not just the family that suffers, but faith itself. The absence of the father casts a shadow over the face of God, and for many, that shadow is all they ever see.

Non Serviam

Have you ever heard the story of the fall of the angels? Long before the fall of man, there was another rebellion — a primal rupture in the order of creation. According to the ancient Franciscan tradition, God revealed to the angels his plan to unite himself not to them, but to humanity — creatures of flesh and bone. Even more scandalous, this union would come not through glory but through humility. God would become man, entering the created order through the womb of a woman, taking on the fragility of human nature, and submitting himself to suffering and death. Faced with this mystery, the angelic host was split.

One of the most radiant among them, a great angel of light, could not bear it. Lucifer — whose very name meant "light-bearer" — refused to serve a God who would stoop so low. He would not bow before this future incarnate Christ, nor would he adore a God who descended into weakness. And so, with a voice that shook the heavens, he declared his revolt: *Non serviam.* I will not serve. With that, a third of the heavenly host fell with him — cast down, not because they lacked power or beauty, but because they could not accept a love that humbled itself.

And so it was that the first being to fall was not a man at all. It was an angel who refused to serve, who preferred pride to love, and self-exaltation to self-gift. And ever since, his words echo in the hearts of fallen men. The dominant man, puffed up with false strength, says *I will not serve* — not my wife, not my children, not anyone. The distant man, curled up in passivity, says the same thing with his silence. He refuses to lead, to protect, to sacrifice. One man rebels with his fists, the other with his absence. But in the depths of each heart, beneath the bravado or behind the retreat, is the same ancient cry: *Non serviam.* I will not serve.[13]

C. S. Lewis put it with piercing observation: "There are only two kinds of people in the end: those who say to God, 'Thy will be done,' and those to whom God says, in the end, 'Thy will be done.'" The former live in a paradise of God's design. The latter live in a hell of their own design. Adam's fall was not just disobedience — it was self-deification. And the ruin that followed was not arbitrary punishment, but the natural collapse of a soul designed to live as a creature (not a creator).

This is the heart of Adam's fall: not merely disobedience, but the attempt to become the source of his own reality. He no longer received meaning from God — he tried to generate it from within himself. Adam, scorning the command he had been given, became jealous of God's prerogatives. In doing so, he established a pattern that would ripple through every generation: men grasping to define reality on their own terms. Indeed, there are only two ways to live: to receive or to grasp. He who receives molds his life according to a reality established by a being outside himself. He accepts his garden, then embraces it for all it is worth, reveling in his fields, plants, animals, and ultimately his woman. His whole existence is an exclamation, "Thy will be done!" In contrast, he who insists on creating his own reality refuses the gift and attempts to usurp the throne. And as was the case with Adam, God replies, "Then thy will be done." In rejecting the terms of the Garden, Adam grasped at a reality of his own making — and that reality, severed from grace, was far different, and far darker, than the one he had been given in Eden.

Echoing the ancient *non serviam* of Satan, and the silence of Adam, many men still follow the path of distance or dominance. My friend Joshua Broome walked that path for a time. Pornography, after all, is a Luciferian blend of both dominance and distance. The one who uses pornography uses a woman through a screen — never asking her permission, never offering relationship — while remaining safely detached.

But after years in that world, Joshua said, "No more." He became a soldier in the fight for human dignity — he speaks to thousands about Christ, advocates on Capitol Hill to expose the dark underbelly of the porn industry, and leads a national ministry. He decided not to let his past hold him back. Maybe what is most inspiring to me is that, despite hundreds of explicit videos that will live forever online, Joshua became a faithful husband and a devoted father to several young boys. If Joshua Broome can sever ties with his sin, if he can overcome the wounds of his absent father, so can you.

CHAPTER 4

New Adams

There are moments in a man's life when he stands exposed — stripped of excuses, defenses, and pretense. No cleverness can hide his sin. No swagger can cover his shame. He stands before another, caught in the act, and everyone knows it. It's in that moment that a man either breaks or is remade.

Victor Hugo gives us such a moment in *Les Misérables*, and it may be one of the most profound portraits of masculine redemption ever written.

After nineteen years in prison, Jean Valjean emerges a hardened man. His body is free, but his heart remains in chains. Bitterness has shaped his soul. He carries the physical brand mark of his past everywhere he goes, and he knows how the world sees him: as a dangerous outcast, a man unworthy of trust or dignity. His very identity has been reduced to a number: 24601.

Then, one cold night, Valjean arrives at the home of Bishop Myriel — an old man of God who opens his doors to the stranger, feeds him, and gives him shelter. For a brief moment, Valjean receives the kindness of a true father. But when the bishop goes to bed, Valjean cannot accept the gift. His soul is still ruled by survival, not trust. So Valjean steals the bishop's silver. He slips quietly into the night, carrying with him not just silverware but the weight of his own shame. But he is caught, of course. The police find him and drag him back to the bishop's door, silver in hand. And there, in the courtyard of the bishop's home, Jean Valjean stands face to face with the truth of who he is.

Anyone who has battled addiction will recognize this moment. Imagine the man who's just finished rehab, determined to start over. He's clean for a day or two, maybe a week. But then the pull of his old life returns, stronger than he thought. He takes the drink, clicks on the porn site, rolls the dice, takes the hit. And the next morning, there he is again: caught, exposed, ashamed. The thought comes crashing in: Maybe I am nothing more than prisoner 24601.

That is exactly where Valjean stands. He knows he is guilty. He knows he deserves the punishment that's coming. And more than anything, he knows that the bishop sees him — fully sees him — and what he has done. It is not just the law that has caught him; it is love. And love knows the truth.

This is the agony of shame. Shame is not merely guilt for what a man has done. It is the terror of being seen in his failure, fully exposed before the eyes of another. It is the urge to flee, to deny, to strike back — or to shrink into despair.

But Bishop Myriel does something that rewrites the script.

Instead of condemnation, he offers grace. He tells the officers that the silver was a gift. Then, to Valjean's shock, he adds:

"Ah! Here you are! I am glad to see you. Well, but how is this? I gave you the candlesticks too, which are of silver like the rest, and for which you can certainly get two hundred francs. Why did you not carry them away with your forks and spoons?"[1]

And with that, he hands Valjean the silver candlesticks, the most precious items in the house.

Then, looking directly into Valjean's eyes, the bishop speaks words that will haunt the man for the rest of his life:

"Forget not, never forget, that you have promised me to use this silver to become an honest man. Jean Valjean, my brother, you no longer belong to evil but to good. It is your soul that I buy from you; I withdraw it from dark thoughts and the spirit of perdition, and I give it to God."[2]

But it is not just a pardon. It is a commission. In that moment, the bishop shoulders the cost of Valjean's sin. He lets the thief go free — not because he is blind to the betrayal, but because he sees something deeper. He sees the man Valjean could become if someone would dare to entrust him with his own redemption.

This is the pattern of Christ. To redeem a man, you must first see him fully — his sin, his shame, his potential — and then meet him with a love that costs you something. Not cheap forgiveness. Not moral grandstanding. But a mercy that comes with a burden, a mercy that risks being wounded.

For Valjean, this encounter becomes the turning point of his life. He will wrestle with it for days, haunted and enlivened by the fact that he was seen, forgiven, and entrusted with dignity all in the same breath. The bishop's mercy breaks through the armor that he had forged to survive. And through that breach, grace begins to work. Jean Valjean spends the rest of his life living out of that interior experience of the redemption offered him by the bishop. What happened for Valjean that day animates the rest of his earthly existence.

Jean Valjean's story is not just the tale of one man. It is the story of all men. Sin isolates us. Shame paralyzes us. Mercy restores. That is what the bishop does for Valjean: He sees his failure, absorbs the cost, and sends him back into the world with a new name, a new identity, and a new task. This is the pattern of redemption itself — the story of Adam, the fall of man, and the coming of Christ to set the broken order right.

At the dawn of the human story, the first Adam was placed in a garden. His task was not abstract. He was charged with ordering the world around him — tilling the soil, naming the creatures, loving the woman. But Adam stopped trusting. He disobeyed. And when he fell, the garden unraveled, the woman stumbled, and the collapse spread throughout all humanity. But God was not content to leave his world in ruins. In the fullness of time, Christ — the New Adam — came to reclaim what was lost. Humanity was lost in a garden. It is only fitting that the rescue began in one too.

The night air outside Jerusalem hung like a veil — heavy with the fragrance of crushed olives and the distant murmur of Passover fires. Jesus stepped beyond the sleeping circle of his friends as if crossing a threshold. It had begun. Moonlight caught the sweat already beading on his brow, a quiet prelude to the storm that would break within. The Garden, once a place of simple retreat, became an arena where the destiny of every human soul converged upon a solitary Man. Gethsemane. Scripture recounts the story as follows:

> He came out, and went, as was his custom, to the Mount of Olives; and the disciples followed him. When he came to the place he said to them, "Pray that you may not come into the time of trial." Then he withdrew from them about a stone's throw, knelt down, and prayed, "Father, if you are willing, remove this cup from me; yet, not my will but yours be done." Then an angel from heaven appeared to him and gave him strength. In his anguish he prayed more earnestly, and his sweat became like great drops of blood falling down on the ground. (Luke 22:39–44)

Fulton Sheen once wrote, "It is very likely that the Agony in the Garden cost him far more suffering than even the physical pain of the crucifixion."[3] According to tradition, it was in Gethsemane that Christ took upon himself the full weight of every sin ever committed in human history. And he did not bear that burden abstractly. He felt it. He entered into the pain of our wrongdoing with faculties not dulled by sin. Unlike us, whose senses have been numbed by guilt and self-deception, Christ's were razor sharp. He experienced the sting of guilt he did not earn, the consequences of crimes he did not commit. Every young man's stinging shame. Every old man's bitter remorse. All of it coursed through the trembling flesh of the Son of God. Christ felt the full weight of every human sin — immediate, personal, searing. This is what happened in Gethsemane. In the garden where the first Adam fled, the New Adam knelt. And from bended knee, through blood and tears, Jesus said, "Not my will but yours be done" (Lk 22:42).

I want to begin with Gethsemane for two reasons. First, because the garden of Gethsemane is an accessible place for meeting Christ in prayer. And second, because what happened in that garden forms the foundation upon which real masculinity is built.

Let us start with the first. Think for a moment of your place of greatest shame. What fruit did you reach for? What forbidden, unspeakable thing did you grasp in the dark? Perhaps your sins are loud — flagrant, unforgettable, still echoing in your memory. Or perhaps they are quiet, buried under layers of practiced silence. Maybe they happened long ago. Maybe they happened this morning. Wherever they live in your soul, call them to mind now.

If you had asked Adam — the first man — about his place of greatest shame, he would have told you about a garden. He would have spoken in halting words about a tree, a serpent, a moment of grasping that cost him and his family everything. He was given a world without suffering, and in a single act, he ruined it. Imagine carrying that weight. Imagine waking each morning knowing your disobedience opened the floodgates to death and loss for every child yet to come. If Adam ever returned to that garden, I suspect he would fall to his knees in tears.

When Christ knelt in Gethsemane, it was as though he stepped through time into that ancient garden to meet Adam ...and to meet you. Maybe your garden is a courtroom where you signed some papers and watched your marriage disappear. Maybe it's a cubicle where ambition slowly displaced your soul. Maybe it's a dark room where you traded romance with a real woman for pixels on a screen. Maybe it's a conversation you can't undo. Maybe it's a debt you can't pay. Whatever your place looks like, Christ wants to meet you there. He wants to receive the shame of your Eden in the garden of Gethsemane, then take it with him to die on the cross.

For some reason, I find Christ more approachable in Gethsemane than at Golgotha. There is something about the garden at night — the shadows, the stillness, the solitude. It feels like a confessional. A place to whisper what I have never said aloud. A place where the Son of God kneels in anguish — not to condemn you, but to level with you, then redeem you, in the same way that the bishop redeemed Valjean. Show him the courtroom, the cubicle, the conversation. He will not flinch. He already knows.

Time and again, I have seen man's journey with God follow the same pattern. A man sins. He does something — perhaps for the thousandth time — that he cannot bear to admit, not to others, perhaps not even to himself. So he hides. He spends his days skirting the memory, keeping it at bay. Then one day, by some act of grace, he finds the strength to face it, surrender it to the Lord, and allow Jesus to transform it. Because men are by nature protectors, their hiding places tend to be well-fortified.

Their shame-stricken memories sit behind thick walls, guarded like a fortress. The journey begins the moment a man dares to open the gate.

What does that look like? Opening the gate looks like prayer. It looks like inviting a close-knit group of friends into a painful subject. It looks like talking with a pastor. It looks like reconciling with someone you have wronged. The details are always unique to the circumstance — but whatever it looks like for you, take the step.

My own experience has involved meeting the Lord in Gethsemane time and time again. There, I have shown him memory after memory. Embarrassment after humiliation after failure. There, in Gethsemane, the trees which once offered me a place to hide become the place of unity with my God. And THAT is the great paradox of sin — that although sin initially divides us from God, repentance is an occasion for a deeper unity. Christ has a brilliant way of transforming our hiding places into spaces for encounter.

Reclaiming the Garden

In his novel *That Hideous Strength*, C. S. Lewis presents Jane Studdock as a character who embodies the spirit of our age. Jane is a young academic who, shaped by skepticism and burdened by suspicion, has made an adversary of men in general and of her husband in particular. Near the story's end, Jane is confronted by a Christlike figure, Ransom, whose quiet strength unsettles her defenses. With gentle firmness, Ransom names the deeper struggle of her heart, showing her that the problem is not her husband but masculinity itself — and, ultimately, the God who fashioned masculinity, imprinting part of his own mystery in its design. Ransom says to her plainly:

> You are offended by the masculine itself: the loud, ir-

> ruptive, possessive thing — the gold lion, the bearded bull — which breaks through hedges and scatters the little kingdom of your primness as the dwarfs scattered the carefully made bed. … But the masculine none of us can escape. What is above and beyond all things is so masculine that we are all feminine in relation to it. You had better agree with your adversary quickly.[4]

Christ in Gethsemane plays the same role for us as Ransom does for Jane. While God meets us in the garden with gentleness, we must remember that the trembling, bloody Christ in Gethsemane is compelling because he holds colossal strength. Jesus in Gethsemane is the God who spoke a word and worlds were born (see Gn 1:3; Ps 33:9). He is the Lord whose right hand shattered armies and split the sea in two (Ex 14:21–22; 15:6). It is he who commanded the sun to stand still in the sky (Jos 10:12–14) and whose voice thunders with such force that the earth itself melts (Ps 29:4; 46:6). He is the God who counts the stars and calls them by name (Is 40:26), who with a single breath can lay low the mightiest empire (2 Kgs 19:35). The blazing majesty of his power was the backdrop against which he chose to bend low, take on flesh, and allow himself to be crushed for our sake. That is what makes Gethsemane so profound: Christ is that kind of man, yet he kneels. His gentleness is striking only because it comes from someone powerful.

This is the Christian story: the God whose power defies description, yet who stoops to meet humanity in Gethsemane. Men are called to be a living icon of that mystery. Men and women should celebrate that calling. Any voice — whether man, woman, or ideology — that says otherwise speaks against a divine design. After Christ meets us in the garden, he does something else the following day: He goes to die at Golgotha. That same night, after the encounter in Gethsemane, the Lord of the universe allows himself to undergo a sham trial. By morning he is handed over to the authorities, scourged within an inch of his life, crowned with thorns, and mocked in a purple robe. Then Pilate presents him to the crowd and utters words with meaning beyond his own understanding: "Here is the man" (Jn 19:5).

Saint Augustine sees this moment as a proclamation of Christ as the New Adam. Just as Moses lifted up the bronze serpent so Israel could be healed, so now Pilate lifts Christ before the world. Behold him and be healed. Behold him and see the true Man, the one who restores humanity by obedience where Adam fell by rebellion.[5]

St. John Chrysostom notes Pilate's intent to defuse the crowd's fury: "Look at Him! Beaten, humiliated, harmless — is this the one you fear?" Yet the purple robe and the thorns, meant as mockery, reveal the true royalty beneath. In the broken, bloodied Christ, kingship is not destroyed but redefined.[6] To behold Christ in this hour is to behold humanity as God designed it: not the grasping of Adam, but the surrender of the New Adam. Pilate spoke in jest, but heaven heard a proclamation. *Ecce Homo.* Behold the true Man.

From there, the soldiers laid the rough wood upon his shoulders and drove him toward Calvary. Step by step, the Lord of glory carried the instrument of his own execution until, at last, he was nailed to it and breathed his final breath.

Here the contrast with Eden is palpable. Adam hid. He blamed. He ran. But when the New Adam came, he did not run from the voice of the Father. He returned to the garden and answered it. In Gethsemane he said, "Not my will but yours be done" (Lk 22:42). That sentence is the axis on which redeemed masculinity turns.

Whereas Adam, in small-minded disobedience, hid behind the trees (see Gn 3:8), Christ, in manly obedience, allowed himself to be impaled on a tree. And there — stretched out, staked across wooden beams — he gives us back our dignity. Like Bishop Myriel before Valjean, he meets us in our failure, but at a far greater cost.

This is the heart of our faith. The basic path of the Christian life is the imitation of Christ. As Jesus himself declares in the Gospel: "Whoever does not bear his own cross and come after me, cannot be my disciple" (Lk 14:27). The imitation of Christ requires more than gentleness. If Christ had not been dangerous, the Romans would never have killed him. Christ did not die to make you quiet; he bled so that you might recover your voice. He spent himself at Calvary so that you might regain your strength. Every masculine passion must be placed in service to the God of Love. Anything else is a fake gospel.

The paradox of Christ in the Gospels is that he is at once all-powerful and perfectly meek. He overturns tables at the temple yet gathers children in his arms. He confronts tyrants and consoles lepers. He breaks stereotypes but holds to tradition. His message is as ancient as it is new. Like Christ, truly great men are essentially paradoxical. They blend realities which appear contradictory but are in fact harmonious. They taste God's magnanimity and savor his humility. Only by holding these together do we reflect the Christ we claim to follow.

Joseph's Masculinity

In his humility, God ordained that a mortal man — Saint Joseph — would serve as Christ's earthly father. The obedience Christ would later display in Gethsemane he first learned in Nazareth, obeying a man whose virtue reflected that of God the Father. Joseph therefore stands as the model for all fathers. Yet, for many years, Joseph meant very little to me.

I will never forget sitting in the chapel at Mundelein Seminary, just north of Chicago. It was a quiet, crystalline morning — the kind of stillness that seems to invite the soul to listen. The rector, Father John, was delivering a homily on the Blessed Virgin Mary, and his words pierced through the silence with uncommon clarity. He spoke of Mary as the model for all human holiness and of her Annunciation as the pinnacle of that holiness. "There was no single, more productive action in human history," he said, "than Mary's receiving the will of God at the Annunciation." The line landed like thunder. But I'll admit that my heart sank. I sat in that pew, gripped by a quiet unease: "Is that what holiness looks like for me?" After all, I cannot conceive divine life in my womb. Sure, Mary's yes was inspiring, but also profoundly feminine. I was left wondering: Is receptivity an exclusively feminine quality? Or is there a masculine mirror image?

There is. And his name is Joseph.

If Mary reveals the feminine face of receptivity in salvation history, then Joseph stands quietly, powerfully, as her masculine counterpart. Matthew's Gospel records an angel appearing to Joseph and bidding him to take Mary as his wife. Like Mary, Joseph receives an annunciation.[7] But, unlike Mary, he says nothing in reply. His yes is not spoken — it is enacted. Joseph "did as the angel of the Lord commanded him" (Mt 1:24).

This is the template of masculine receptivity: It listens, receives direction, and then acts. Joseph does not passively wait for confirmation or explanation. He rises. He leads. He protects. He builds. He becomes a guardian of the Holy Family, not by grasping at something outside God's will, but by accepting God's call and bending his life around its demands.

Joseph's sensitivity to the will of God becomes the guiding star of his entire life. Through the lens of obedience, every masculine task — every burden borne, every decision made, every act of provision or protection — takes on a new splendor. Nowhere is this more evident than in the life of Saint Joseph. In all three of his recorded actions in Matthew's Gospel, Joseph's activity is preceded by divine instruction. First, at his own annunciation, the angel tells him: "Joseph, son of David, do not be afraid to take Mary your wife, for the child conceived in her is from the Holy Spirit" (Mt 1:20). Second, after Jesus is born, an angel commands: "Get up, take the child and his mother, and flee to Egypt" (Mt 2:13). Finally, after Herod's death: "Get up, take the child and his mother, and go to the land of Israel" (Mt 2:20). In each case, Joseph acts decisively. He leads. He moves. He protects. But only after he listens. Only after he receives.

It is only through the lens of obedience that we could ever understand the Church's teaching on headship. The Lord teaches us in Ephesians 5 that a husband is the head of his family. The key text reads as follows: "Wives, be subject to your husbands as you are to the Lord. For the husband is the head of the wife as Christ is the head of the church, the body of which he is the Savior" (Eph 5:22–23). To our modern ears, such a command may sound repressive, but cast against the backdrop of the Gospel, it is the opposite.

The key to understanding male headship is viewing it within the context of a truly Christian marriage. Outside of that context, it makes no sense. Within authentically *Christian* marriage, headship presupposes that a husband lives his life in intimate obedience to the will of the Father. It also presupposes that a husband is, as Saint Paul says later, loving his wife "as Christ loved the church and gave himself up for her, in order to make her holy" (Eph 5:25–26). A man who loves his wife in this way wakes each morning ready to lay down his life for his bride. Finally, headship presupposes that a husband is in deep communication with his wife. As a person also made in God's image and likeness and in possession of her own volition, she obeys not as a slave, but as a person and friend.[8] In this sense, Mary follows Joseph as a companion, not a servant.[9] This is the Christian vision of male headship: the image of a man imitating Christ by laying down his life daily for his bride and a bride joyfully receiving his leadership.

The Holy Family is the guiding light for understanding headship. Joseph's authority was real. Mary and Jesus followed his lead in the flight to Egypt and in their return from it. Mary, for her part, received Joseph's headship not as a diminishment of her dignity but as the proper ordering of their communion. She, who had already said her *fiat* to God, now entrusted herself to Joseph's care, confident that his obedience to the Father would secure her path. In this interplay, the mystery of Ephesians 5 comes alive: The husband initiates by laying down his life in costly love and the wife magnifies that gift through trusting acceptance. Headship is thus revealed as an icon of Christ's own love for the Church.

In the final analysis, all true leadership requires obedience, in and outside the family. A soldier is only as good as his willingness to obey orders. A president is only worthy of the office if he honestly reads the signs of the times, discerns what is best for his people, and submits to the demands of justice and truth. An entrepreneur succeeds not by imposing his will on the market, but by perceiving its realities — its needs, limits, and opportunities — and acting in accord with them. Leadership, then, is not domination. It is a form of receptive action: first accepting reality as it is, then moving decisively in response.

The greater the leader's ability to accept factors beyond his control — whether in the battlefield, the boardroom, or the human heart — and communicate those realities to others, the greater his capacity to lead well. Any form of leadership that neglects this — leadership that refuses to listen, refuses to receive, refuses to obey the truth of the situation — is a hollow counterfeit. It requires the leader to swiftly discard how he wants reality to be, sacrificing his desire to live in a fiction. This kind of leadership demands a daily death to ego. Instead, he must shoulder the burden of truth and act accordingly. In this, every good leader echoes Christ in Gethsemane: "Not my will but yours be done" (Lk 22:42).

The heart of Joseph's leadership was forged not only within the family but also in the dignity of his labor. Scripture tells us very little about Joseph. But Matthew 13:55 does tell us that he was a carpenter. That simple fact bears immense weight. Joseph's work was not a background detail to his holiness. Rather, it was one of its primary expressions. So too must men today put their hands to the garden entrusted to us, every facet of it. The risk-accepting, world-building instincts of Adam must be brought to bear on every dimension of the modern workplace. The world needs rugged men in the trades — plumbers, electricians, carpenters — who mend what is broken and build what endures. It needs fierce advocates in the courts who defend justice without flinching and bold entrepreneurs who shoulder risk, forge teams, and create jobs. It needs warriors of beauty — writers, artists, and filmmakers — who wield their creativity with integrity. It needs men of science who bring precision to technology, doctors who fight for health in dignity, teachers who embolden young minds, and leaders in every sphere who steward power with humility and strength. None of this is small. None of it is soft. This is masculine leadership in action. Like Joseph, we are summoned not to speak endlessly about what must be done, but to take up the tools placed in our hands and build.

Is this how you lead? Do you live in the real world, or do you inflate reality to suit your desires? Do you serve the actual needs of the people who follow you, or the version of their needs that flatters your image? Does your reading of the world involve setting your self-interest aside, or is it a veiled, egotistical self-assertion?

The New Adam

In a Holy Saturday homily long attributed to St. John Chrysostom, Christ speaks as the New Adam who sleeps in death, and from his pierced side a new Eve is brought forth. Just as Eve was formed from Adam's rib in the first garden, so too the Church — Christ's Bride — is born from his side, flowing with blood and water. From this wound, the Church pours forth.[10] From this wound, the Bride emerges, not clothed in shame or fig leaves, but in glory and grace.

Christ goes to the cross not merely to die, but to give himself to the Father and to give his Bride to the world. In the tree of Eden, man was divided from God. On the tree of Calvary, man is joined to God again. And from this second tree, love flows outward: A Bride is formed, a Church is born, and the gates of paradise, long shut, are thrown wide open.

Christ did not simply pass through Gethsemane and ascend from the cross into glory. He continued downward into the stillness of death, into the silence of the tomb. And Scripture is not content to let an important detail go unnoticed: "Now in the place where he was crucified there was a garden, and in the garden a new tomb" (Jn 19:41). A garden. The story comes full circle. As Adam once fell asleep in Eden, so Christ slept in his tomb in the resurrection garden.

And when he rose, it was no accident that the first place he appeared was a garden where Mary Magdalene waited, weeping. Ancient voices like Hippolytus and Ambrose saw Mary Magdalene as a type for the New Eve: not because she caused the fall, but because she is the first to behold the Risen Christ, the first to hear him speak her name, the first to be sent as a witness to the apostles.[11]

The scriptures record that, after Christ's burial, Mary Magdalene stood loyally by, weeping outside the tomb. She who was once possessed by seven demons, she who loved Jesus with unashamed devotion, now found herself alone again. Her Lord was gone. Her hope, entombed. "Woman, why are you weeping?" came the voice behind her, and still she does not recognize him (Jn 20:15). The weight of sin, sorrow, and disappointment can cloud the eyes. Augustine says that Mary looked for the dead among the dead and could not yet see Life itself standing before her.[12] Gregory the Great called it love's blindness: She longed so deeply for Jesus that she could not imagine his triumph.[13]

And what happened next? She mistook him for the gardener. But she was not wrong. He is the Gardener. He is the New Adam, come to tend not just Eden, but the whole cosmos. He spoke her name — "Mary" — and in that moment, her blindness broke. The voice that calmed storms and cast out demons had called her by name, and she knew him. The risen Christ gazed upon her not as Adam once looked at Eve with delight, but with a gaze more piercing, more healing. Christ beamed over Mary not only as divine lover but also as creator and redeemer! Adam beheld Eve and rejoiced in her likeness. Christ beheld Mary and restored her dignity. His gaze affirmed not just her, but all fallen humanity. The garden had been reclaimed, and the Gardener stood risen in its midst.

We asked in the second chapter: Are the things of your life about the people of your life? That question must return here, sharper and more urgent. It is not enough to work hard. It is not enough to be generally faithful. The question is: Does your strength serve your relationships? Are you cultivating your home, your calendar, your body, your attention, for the good of your bride and your children? Is the work of your life ordered to the people of your life? Christ, the New Adam, did for Mary what the first Adam failed to do for Eve. He protected her. He harnessed his strength. He stood in harm's way. And in the safety produced by his sacrifice, he affirmed her. He called her by her name.

That is the picture of masculinity we are called to imitate. As men who follow the New Adam, we are summoned to more than material provision and protection. We are called to enter, with permission, the intimate worlds of our wives and children — to affirm them, to play with them, to feed them emotionally and spiritually.

So, husbands, are you guarding and savoring your wife in all the dimensions of her being? And what of your children? Do you stoop down, look them in the eye, and say, "I'm proud of you"? If you do not yet have children, are you cultivating now the emotional intelligence that will one day make you a great husband and father? You were made to be a cultivator, not just of income or achievements, but of people. That is the final test of a man's garden: not what it produces, but who and how it nourishes.

Don't be afraid to take the first step. Remember that at every stage of human history, some vital aspect of Christianity comes under attack. In the early Church, it was the central dogmas of the faith: the Incarnation, the Trinity, the divinity of Christ. When a Christian teaching is threatened, that is, of course, a cause for concern — but it is also a cause for excitement. Why? Because truth always wins. Truth has a way of emerging from conflict more radiant. When Christian doctrine is challenged, the battle often acts like a chisel to stone — striking, yes, but also clearing away the grime and revealing the brilliance beneath. That is why we have beautiful treatises on the Trinity and the Incarnation from the early Church Fathers. Controversy carved out clarity.

Today, the crisis centers on men and masculinity. There is a call for men to become men again, but not by turning back the clock to a photocopy of their grandfathers. What we need is not a nostalgic return to some old version of manhood, but the renewal of an ancient picture of masculinity. We need men who will stand as living icons of the New Adam.

And when the world encounters these new men, I suspect, and I hope, that the world's reaction will mirror that of Mary Magdalene at the tomb: perhaps perplexity at first, but then recognition and joy that what once was lost has been redeemed.

CHAPTER 5

Dads and the Domestic Church

When Franz Jägerstätter kissed his daughters goodbye for the last time, he knew exactly what he was leaving them — and what he wasn't.

He would not be there to guide them through adolescence or teach them how to work the hillside farms of Saint Radegund. He would not share in their birthdays, help them solve life's daily problems, or walk them down the aisle at their weddings. His absence would wound them. His execution would break their hearts.

And yet Jägerstätter went to his death freely, deliberately, and with his eyes wide open.

Why? Because for him, there was one duty of fatherhood that stood above all others: to bear witness to the faith. Not just to speak of it, but to live it, and, if necessary, to die for it.

When the Nazis conscripted him to serve in their military machine, Jägerstätter refused. Quietly but resolutely, he told his wife, his friends, and his pastor: "I cannot and may not take an oath in favor of a government that is fighting an unjust war." Local villagers called him a fool. Some priests urged him to think again. After all, wasn't he a husband and father? Didn't he owe it to his family to survive?

But Jägerstätter saw it differently. To him, the deepest betrayal would not be death but apostasy. What good is a father's provision if it comes at the cost of his soul? What value is a father's presence if it teaches cowardice?

He wrote to his wife Franziska from prison, explaining that many tried to burden his conscience by reminding him of his responsibilities to her and the children. But for Jägerstätter, the real burden — the heavier, generational burden — would be leaving his daughters with the burden of the memory of a father who betrayed his own faith. For Jägerstätter, better a father who died a witness to Christ than one who lived as a coward.[1]

This chapter is about that kind of fatherhood, a kind not defined merely by material provision or daily presence, but by faithful witness. A father's first duty is not simply to raise children who believe in God, but to model for them what it looks like to follow God when it costs something. Children learn faith from their father's words, but they are formed even more deeply by his witness.

During my years as a graduate student, I was always searching for anchor points — truths about men and masculinity that could stand firm in an age of cultural drift. These are hard to find. Nearly every claim about what it means to be a man is up for debate, and the most basic questions about fatherhood or masculinity often spark controversy.

But as I dug deeper into the research, particularly the literature on men and faith, one truth kept rising to the surface.

Across studies, across generations, across cultures, the pattern was unmistakable: fathers have an outsized influence on the spiritual lives of their children. More than mothers. More than schools. More than churches. A father's witness — his presence or absence, his faith or faithlessness — often sets the trajectory for his children's faith for the rest of their lives. Franz Jägerstätter knew this long before any sociologist put it in a study. That's why he refused to leave his daughters the legacy of a father who had compromised his conscience. His sacrifice wasn't just about his own faith — it was about theirs.

In the last several decades, study after study has confirmed a simple, stubborn truth: The outward witness of a father's faith is critically important for passing on faith to the next generation. One of the most rigorous examples is a four-decade longitudinal study published by Oxford University Press. Researchers followed 350 families and over 3,000 individuals across multiple generations, seeking to uncover the secret to successful religious transmission. The findings of the study showed that there is a stronger correlation between children and the faith practices of their fathers and grandfathers than mothers and grandmothers.[2]

In other words, if a father is active and engaged with his children, they are far more likely to make his faith their own. Newer research confirms this pattern. Among the most recent is Communio's "Nationwide Study on Faith and Relationships" (2023), which gathered data from 19,000 Christian families across denominational lines. The report's conclusion is blunt: "The sharp and culturally disruptive decline in married fathers over the past 60 years appears to be driving the decline in active church participation on a societal level over the past 40 years."[3]

The statistics paint a clear and unsettling picture: Faithful fathers are one of the best predictors of faithful children. Unfortunately, in today's world, there aren't enough of them. For decades, sociologists and religious researchers have observed a consistent pattern: Women are more active in religious life than men. According to a 2016 Pew Research Center study, in Christian-majority countries — including the United States — 53% of women reported attending religious services weekly, compared to 46% of men.[4] This gap extends beyond church attendance to practices like daily prayer, devotional life, and the importance placed on faith. More recently, the 2023–24 "Pew Religious Landscape Study" confirmed that this disparity persists. Across nearly every measure of religious involvement, women continue to outpace men, making the gender gap in religious practice one of the most stable patterns in modern religious sociology.[5]

The disparity goes beyond private devotion or Sunday worship. In the day-to-day life of most churches, it is women who do the bulk of the labor. This trend plays out across most denominations, but to give a poignant example, studies estimate that up to 85% of non-ordained roles in Catholic parishes are held by women — including religious education for youth, volunteer leadership, pastoral care, and ministry coordination. Whether teaching catechism classes, leading Bible studies, or organizing outreach events, women disproportionately serve as the hands and feet of church life.[6]

My personal experiences and research have confirmed two truths. First, a father's faith is among the strongest predictors of whether his children will remain faithful. Exceptions abound — I know devout, exceptional fathers whose children have still left the Church — but the data is clear: Fathers matter profoundly. Second, for decades now, women have carried a disproportionate share of responsibility in church life across nearly every denomination. This is no fault of women; ideally, men and women would serve together. The real problem arises when men abdicate their role, leaving the Church with a distinctly feminine character. Taken together, these realities reveal not only a crisis for the Church today but an even greater crisis for the Church of tomorrow.

Keeping this reality in mind, I urge not only fathers but also single men to take their role seriously. The witness of a man's faith carries enormous weight. Fathers and grandfathers hold a place of primacy, but their voices need reinforcement. A father's words echo more deeply when a grandfather affirms them, and children are often more likely to embrace their father's example when they see it corroborated in the lives of single uncles, godfathers, and family friends.

Men and the Church in the Home

Why are fathers so pivotal when it comes to the transmission of faith? That question can be answered from many angles — psychological, sociological, historical, even political. Each of those perspectives is valuable, and much could be said from each angle. But here, I want to offer a theological answer, because if we fail to grasp the spiritual dimension of this question, we miss the deepest truth.

Let's begin with the most fundamental Christian prayer: the "Our Father." The Gospel of Matthew recounts how this prayer was first taught. The apostles had watched Jesus pray, and they recognized something different in his relationship to God — something intimate, direct, and powerful. So they asked him plainly, and he responded by teaching them this prayer: "Our Father who art in heaven, / hallowed be thy name. / Your kingdom come. / Your will be done, / on earth as it is in heaven. / Give us this day our daily bread. / And forgive us our debts, / as we also have forgiven our debtors. / And do not bring us to the time of trial, / but rescue us from the evil one" (Mt 6:9–13).

Notice that Jesus doesn't begin with abstract theology. He teaches them to begin with relationship, specifically, with the word "Father." From the very beginning of Christian revelation, the primary address believers are invited to use with God is "Father." This is not a peripheral or symbolic detail; it is foundational.

The identity of God is revealed to humanity first and foremost in the language of fatherhood.

So when we ask, "Why are fathers so crucial to faith?", the answer is not only sociological. It is theological. The role of the father is written into the very structure of Christian revelation. Faith is not passed on primarily through lectures or programs, but through relationship — through fatherhood, both divine and human. To be a Christian is to be in relationship with Christ. To be the father you were created to be, a man needs to know God the Father.

The importance of a father's role in passing on the faith is not just a sociological observation. It derives from creation, itself, as evidenced by the biblical tradition. The ancient Israelites understood this with profound clarity. In the Hebraic worldview, the male — or *zakar* — was seen as the bearer of spiritual memory, the keeper and transmitter of religious identity. The *zakar*'s role wasn't merely biological or economic; it was spiritual and communal. He was responsible for remembering God's works and ensuring the memory of them was passed from generation to generation, so that Israel never forgot who they were or to whom they belonged.

This calling was not left to chance. God designed specific religious rites and traditions to embed this responsibility into the very structure of Israelite life. Many of these rituals were not led by priests at the Temple but by fathers, in the home, at the family table, and with their own hands.

Consider circumcision, which was first commanded in Genesis 17:10. On the surface, it may seem puzzling that such a physical, intimate act would be tied to the cosmic story of salvation. But circumcision was more than a bodily sign — it was a mark cut into the flesh as a permanent reminder of the covenant between God and his people. And where was this mark placed? On the generative organ. This signaled that the covenant wasn't just personal; it was generational. It was about passing on life and faith together.

Importantly, the act of circumcision was not performed by temple priests or religious officials. It was a father-led ritual, taking place in the home. The father was the one who physically enacted this sign upon his son, binding his family to the covenant and marking himself as a link in the chain of faith from past to future.[7]

Then there is the Passover, the most important feast in the Israelite calendar (see Ex 12). The Passover commemorated Israel's liberation from slavery in Egypt and the night when the angel of death "passed over" the houses marked by the blood of the lamb. For generations, Jews have celebrated this feast through a meal known as the Seder, which retells the story of Israel's deliverance. The father again leads this ritual. He presides over the Passover table, explaining the meaning of each article of food, telling the story of the Exodus, and answering the questions of his children. The Passover meal was not just about ritual observance — it was about embedding the story of salvation into the hearts of the next generation. And the father's role was essential.

A third example is the rite of the firstborn, found in Exodus 13 and echoed in Luke 2:22–24 when Joseph and Mary present Jesus in the Temple. In ancient Israel, the firstborn son held special significance, symbolizing the family's future and the nation's continuation. According to the Old Testament law, the firstborn son belonged to God. But instead of offering him up as a sacrifice (as was the custom of some of the pagan people in the ancient world), the Hebrew father performed a redemption ritual. He would offer an animal sacrifice to redeem his child, acknowledging that life belongs to God alone. In this act, the father publicly declared both his gratitude and his responsibility: He is the one tasked with safeguarding his child's life and leading that child in covenantal faith.

All these three traditions — circumcision, Passover, and the rite of the firstborn — were essential to the Hebrew faith. They were all family rituals and the father played an indispensable role. This was not accidental or arbitrary. These practices were designed by God to reinforce the father's responsibility as a spiritual leader. It was through the father that the family entered the covenant. It was through the father that the family remembered God's saving acts. It was through the father that the identity of the child was affirmed and consecrated.

Though Christians no longer practice these specific rituals, the principle remains fully intact. The father is still called to be a spiritual leader in the home, a teacher of the faith, and a witness to God's covenantal love. In fact, Augustine considered the father to be akin to the bishop of the family, and in a faithful household, husband and wife worked together to ensure that the faith was passed on to their children. But in today's culture, there is a strong and subtle pressure on men to abdicate that role, to take a spiritual backseat while concerned mothers carry the weight of religious formation. But, as we have seen in the studies above, the father cannot be replaced by the mother.

This is clearly not the biblical model. Children need to see their fathers outwardly committed to their faith. They need to witness their dads praying, teaching, correcting, and encouraging the Faith. The father's role is not optional or secondary. It is central to the passing on of religious identity. The stakes are too high for abdication, silence, or passivity. So what does this mean for you?

For the men reading this book — especially those who call themselves Christian — the biblical significance of fatherhood carries weighty implications. Simply put, you must become a witness to your faith. That witness doesn't have to be complicated. It doesn't require a theology degree or a platform or public recognition.

I began this chapter with the story of Franz Jägerstätter for a reason. Jägerstätter wasn't a scholar or a priest. He wasn't a public figure or a theologian. He was just a dad — a farmer from a small village who refused to compromise his conscience. He stuck to his convictions, and that made all the difference. Decades after his death, director Terrence Malick brought his story to life in the film *A Hidden Life*, portraying Franz as he was: a strong but simple man, rooted in faith, willing to stand firm when it counted. That is the model.

Your children don't need you to have brilliant insights about the Trinity or a Ph.D. in apologetics. But they do need you to think alongside them about the questions that matter. They don't need you to win the Nobel Peace Prize, but it would do them a great good to see you serve the poor with your own hands because of your love of Christ. Your children need to see you pray. Not once in a while. Not just at Christmas or Easter. They need to see prayer woven into your life — simple, consistent, honest prayer. It doesn't have to be complicated or flowery. In fact, it's probably better if it isn't. Most importantly, your children need to see that you too need Christ's forgiveness, that you are not perfect, but that you are trying, step-by-step, to be a faithful disciple of Jesus.

Think again of all those Israelite fathers who, over the ages, have led their families through the annual Passover ritual. Very few were rabbis or scholars. They were just dads, guiding their children through the sacred story, reminding them of who God is and who they were called to be. They pray with their families as fathers because that is their role. Your children also need your witness; they need to see you pray. They need to see you live your faith — not perfectly, but persistently. In this case, consistency and authenticity are more powerful than brilliance.

Priest of Your Domestic Church

After reading study after study about the critical role fathers play in the transmission of faith, I expected to find hope. Instead, I found a crisis. When I began talking to men — real men, not theoretical subjects in surveys — I encountered the same problem repeatedly. Man after man, husband after husband, father after father looked me in the eye and said some version of the same thing: "I have no idea how to lead my family in faith." These weren't apathetic men. They weren't lazy or disinterested. Many of them were hungry to lead. They wanted to step up. But they didn't know how.

I started gathering small groups of men. Some were single, most were married, and many were dads. As we shared stories, one uncomfortable truth kept surfacing: Even the simplest acts of spiritual leadership, like praying before meals or saying bedtime prayers with their children, left many of them anxious, hesitant, or paralyzed. For some, it was because no one had ever shown them how. For others, it was because they carried wounds from their own fathers' silence.

I was a young father myself, asking the same hard questions. So, I set out on a mission — not just a research project, but a personal search for answers. What do faithful fathers actually do to pass the faith from one generation to the next? What makes the difference between a father whose children grow up in the Church and one whose children drift away?

That journey led me through Scripture, through piles of sociological data, and eventually across the country, recording interviews with men who had wrestled with these questions firsthand. I spoke with heroic fathers, seasoned priests, exorcists, psychologists, and scholars. I listened to men who had succeeded and men who had failed. I took notes. I asked hard questions. I prayed.

Eventually, that search became a professionally curated course on faith transmission, built to help men do what so many told me they were afraid to try to do: lead their families in faith. I want to share with you some of the diamonds that emerged in that search — not abstract theories or ideals, but practical, hard-won wisdom about how fathers can pass on the faith in a world that is trying desperately to stop them.

> For those who are fathers or who might be fathers someday, you are the priest of your domestic Church.[8] Pope

St. John Paul II spoke to this theme in a homily in Australia in 1986 during the season of Advent, in which the Church reflects particularly on the Holy Family. He said:

> "The family is the domestic church." The meaning of this traditional Christian idea is that the home is the Church in miniature. The Church is the sacrament of God's love. She is a communion of faith and life. She is a mother and teacher. She is at the service of the whole human family as it goes forward towards its ultimate destiny. In the same way the family is a community of life and love. It educates and leads its members to their full human maturity and serves the good of all along the road of life. The family is the "first and vital cell of society." In its own way it is a living image and historical representation of the mystery of the Church. The future of the world and of the Church, therefore, passes through the family.[9]

Your family is a "church in miniature." You might call it a domestic or "home church," and it is the role of this church, embedded in the wider Church, to cultivate faith in your children.

If the family is truly a "domestic church," what does that mean for how it lives and functions? Most fundamentally, it means that the family shares in the very mission of the wider Church. What the Church is called to do on a grand scale, the family is called to embody in miniature. As the Church serves the poor, so must the family. As the Church proclaims the gospel, so must the family evangelize. As the Church teaches the faith, so must the family be a school of faith.

If you want to hand down a robust and living faith to your

children, where should you start? Should you commit to attending Mass more often? Begin a nightly prayer routine? Send your kids to more retreats or mission opportunities? Should you help them serve the poor or meet their neighbors?

These are all good questions. But for most families, the idea of adding more to an already packed schedule can feel overwhelming from the start. And here's the truth: Handing on the faith is less about adding new tasks to your calendar and more about shaping who your family becomes. Don't get me wrong, all of the most vibrant families that I spoke to did indeed do heroic things for the faith, things like family service to the poor, deep intellectual engagement, family prayer, etc., but the specific practices varied.

Business strategist Peter Drucker once famously said, "Culture eats strategy for breakfast." His point was simple: Organizations succeed not because of clever plans but because of the habits, values, and spirit that permeate their daily life. Families are not companies, but the same principle applies. When it comes to raising children in the faith, family faith culture eats parenting strategy for breakfast.

Think of it like painting a room. Having the right tools — brushes, rollers, paint — is essential. Without them, you won't get far. But anyone who has painted well knows that the difference between a good job and a great one is always in the preparation. Spackling, sanding, taping, dusting — these are the behind-the-scenes steps that make the paint stick. When it comes to passing along the faith, your preparation is your family culture.

So yes, as the priest of your domestic church, you should take great pride in your "tools." Be careful to select the people, the books, and the experiences that will form your child, just like a great craftsman takes pride in his tools. You should indeed bring your kids to catechism classes, encourage good retreats, give kids access to Scripture and sacred art. Those things matter. But tools without preparation won't work. What prepares a child's heart to receive the faith is the culture of the home. Faith is just as much "caught" as it is "taught." Is your home the kind of place where faith feels normal, integrated, and alive?

Earlier I mentioned Vern Bengtson's five-generation study on faith transmission. That research, along with several similar studies, identified common traits in families that successfully passed on their faith. At the heart of Bengtson's findings was one unmistakable conclusion: Fathers play a decisive role in the spiritual formation of their children. The excerpt below makes the point with striking clarity:

> For religious transmission, having a close bond with one's father matters even more than a close relationship with one's mother. Clearly, the quality of a child's relationship with his or her father is important for the internalization of the parents' religious traditions, beliefs, and practices. Emotional closeness with mothers remains important for religious inheritance but not to the same degree as it is for fathers.[10]

Want to pass along the faith to your children? Form emotionally secure bonds with your kids. Bengston's study underscores our point from Chapter Three that among the most damaging things that a father can do to his children is to be emotionally and relationally distant from them. Religious piety alone is not enough. Even if parents set a good example and teach the right beliefs, none of it compensates for a lack of warmth. Adults who describe their childhood homes as "warm" are 27% more likely to remain faithful Christians.[11]

Warmth does not mean mushiness. Children thrive under authoritative parents — those with high but reasonable expectations, who communicate well, show affection, and guide with reason rather than coercion. Ironically, parents who abdicate authority often end up less close to their children. Kids don't need peers; they need guides.[12] Children need fathers who set firm boundaries amidst the context of deep relational bonds.

But when you think about it, isn't this just what God's love looks like? Is he not both firm and affectionate? God corrects his children because he loves them, and he is always ready to embrace them the moment they turn back to him. His discipline is never cruel, never random, and never distant. It always flows from love and leads back to love. That is the model for Christian parenting.

There is far more to say about parenting and good fatherhood than can be covered here. Entire libraries could be filled with books on the subject — many of them written by men more seasoned and experienced than I am. I include the topic in this book because this is a book which paints a picture of the man we are called to become, and if we are going to sketch a true picture of masculine excellence, fatherhood cannot be left out. Even for the man who never has children of his own, this remains true: By virtue of being male, he is called to be a living icon of God's fatherly love. That's not a role you can opt out of. In every community, in every friendship, in every relationship, a man bears that weight, whether he wants to or not.

Let that sink in. As a man — a son of Adam — you stand as an icon of the living God. For those younger than you, for anyone under your influence, and especially for your children, their understanding of God will be shaped, in part, by what they gather from you. They will make inferences about the Father based on the face you show them. That's not sentimental rhetoric; it's reality. Every shred of sociological data I've found confirms this. The way you live, lead, and love matters more than you can imagine. The picture you portray will echo in the minds and hearts of those who watch you.

Now here's the secret: You will fail at this responsibility. And you'll fail frequently. I hate to admit it, but I live every day with the sober knowledge that the witness I give my own children is lacking. It's not just imperfect — it's often woefully insufficient. That's the brutal truth of fatherhood in a fallen world.

So what do we do with that? Let me leave you with two final points. First, don't father alone. You have strengths, and you have deficiencies. The same is true of every man. That's why you need to father alongside a community of good friends. There will be moments when your children don't want to hear the lesson from you, but they may be open to hearing it from another adult they trust. Raising children among a faithful community is not optional; it's essential. Study after study confirms this: Families who immerse themselves in vibrant Christian community and who make faith a normal part of public conversation in the home are far more likely to raise children who keep the faith into adulthood.[13] So form community. Speak openly about your faith. Surround your children with other witnesses.

Second, cultivate humble authenticity. Since you know you will fall short in your witness, don't pretend otherwise. Research shows that the parents who left the most lasting, positive impression were not the flawless ones; they were the ones who were clearly faithful, deeply loving, and — this is key — profoundly humble.[14] They admitted when they were wrong. They apologized. They modeled repentance.[15]

Too often, in the caricatures of the past, the religious man — the so-called "man of God" — was pictured as little more than a strait-laced lawgiver: rigid, distant, emotionally cold. That is the old Adam, or at least one version of him: a man obsessed with rules but blind to relationship, hiding behind control because he fears being vulnerable.

But an icon of the New Adam is different. Yes, he is firm. Yes, he calls his family and his community to be accountable.

But there is more to him than strictness. He is affectionate, not aloof; connected, not isolated; authentic, not performative; humble, not proud. He is willing to confess when he fails. He builds a household and a community where discipline and mercy, truth and tenderness, correction and compassion all coexist.

That's why I include these points here — to help sketch the picture of the New Adam, the man we are all called to become. Whether you're a father or not, if you take up the call to be a Christian man, you take up the call to reflect the fatherhood of God. Your role as priest of your domestic church is not about perfection — it's about presence, sacrifice, and the courage to lead with love.

That is the picture of manhood that will heal our families, transform our communities, and echo into the next generation.

CHAPTER 6

Men for the Kingdom

In the frozen hell of a North Korean prison camp, Fr. Emil Kapaun bent down and lifted a man who could not walk. His legs were broken, his strength gone. The guards had left him in the latrine to die. But Kapaun — gaunt, frostbitten, half-starved himself — hoisted the man onto his back and carried him to safety.

No one had told him to do this. No medal waited. In fact, he had been warned not to intervene. But this was what he did, again and again: carrying the dying, sneaking them food, boiling water in a crushed tin helmet to wash the wounds of men left for dead. Some of them were young and afraid. Some were fathers who longed to see their children again. Many would survive because of him. He prayed over them. He cracked jokes with them. He defied the guards for them. And in the end, he died for them.

Father Kapaun was a Catholic priest. He had no wife, no kids, no house of his own. He died childless, penniless, and unmarried. And yet he fathered thousands. During the process of writing this book, I found myself in Wichita, Kansas — his home diocese. I've returned to visit several times. And what I've seen is a groundswell of devout men, faithful families, strong fathers. There are a lot of reasons why the Church in Wichita is so strong, but one of the reasons is that Wichita has a hero: Father Emil Kapaun.

As a young man, Emil Kapaun did not become less of a man by giving up family life. He became more. In laying down his life for many fathers, he became a father of fathers. And his strength still echoes through the men of his city today.

That is what this chapter is about. The idea that celibacy is somehow "less" masculine is not just wrong — it is destructively wrong. It strips dignity from those who are called to this noble life, and it leaves the men of the Church impoverished in their understanding of masculinity. It treats celibacy as a sterile absence rather than what it truly is: a powerful, generative gift.

In this book we have offered Adam in the garden as the picture of what it means to be a man, a picture that is only brought to completion with the New Adam in the garden of the resurrection. Adam orders the things of the world towards the people of the world. And what happens when Adam comes into union with his person, Eve? He makes more people — he generates life. In this sense, generativity — the capacity to give life — is intimately united to masculinity. Sometimes that life is given biologically. But far more powerful is the life given spiritually: in self-gift, in sacramental ministry, in the steadfast leadership of a parish, a diocese, a community. A man is most masculine not when he takes, but when he gives. And the celibate man — precisely because he has renounced the pleasures and privileges of natural fatherhood — is uniquely free to give himself entirely to the Church and the world. The celibate man puts himself in a uniquely powerful position to generate spiritual life.

Celibacy is not a detour from masculinity, but for those who have been given the grace to receive it, celibacy is a grace-filled fulfillment of masculinity. The priest stands as a bridegroom, a spiritual father, and what I will call an icon for icons. Single men, which includes those called to the priesthood, generate life for their communities in a way that is simply impossible for their married brothers. Not every man is called to celibacy. But every man is called to be a giver of life. And the celibate man, far from being an exception, is often the clearest embodiment of that call.

This chapter is a salute to those men. To the pastors who dispense grace and lead their flocks with quiet courage. To the single men who serve their churches, their friends, their communities with the kind of strength and availability that only celibacy affords. To the saints who laid down their lives — and in doing so, generated life in abundance.

Masculinity and The Priesthood

For a brief season in graduate school, I served as an adjunct professor at St. John Vianney Seminary in Denver, Colorado — an exceptional place by any measure. During that period, I was invited on two separate occasions to deliver an intensive lecture series on the topic of masculinity. The audience wasn't college students, married men, or young professionals. They were seminarians — men preparing to lay down their lives for the Church as Catholic priests.

In those lectures, I unpacked many of the themes that have shaped this book: Adam in the garden, the New Adam, the danger of disordered dominance and distance, and the sacred nature of masculinity. And in both series — almost like clockwork — one young man would raise his hand near the end of the final session and ask, "So what does this mean for me?".

The priest is a man set apart, not because he is less of a man, but because he has been called to embody masculinity in a radical and sacrificial way. At the heart of this calling is a profound paradox: The celibate priest becomes a bridegroom without a wife, a father without children. And this is not a symbolic game. It is a lived, generative reality. The priest's celibacy is not a sterile absence; it is a potent space, a consecrated interior room where the life of God is brought forth, nurtured, and poured out into the world.[1]

First and foremost, the priest is a bridegroom. This is not poetic flourish; it is theological truth. The priest is configured to Christ, who is the Bridegroom of the Church. In the Eucharistic sacrifice, in the preaching of the Word, in the absolution of sins, the priest gives himself entirely to his Bride, the Church. His celibacy does not hinder that self-gift. Rather, it enables it. He is not divided. He belongs wholly to her. This total gift of self, made possible through celibacy, is what allows the priest to become generative in a supernatural way. Just as Adam became generative when united to Eve, the New Adam becomes infinitely more generative in his union with the Church. The priest, standing in the person of Christ, participates in this spousal mystery. He becomes a spiritual father — not of one family, but of many. His is not a lesser fatherhood; it is a magnified one.

But the priest is not only a bridegroom and a father. He is an icon for icons. Every earthly father is an icon of God the Father. His authority, his tenderness, his strength — all of it points beyond himself to the ultimate source. But earthly fathers, for all their dignity, are still broken, still in need of healing and guidance. And it is the priest who fathers the fathers. It is the priest who listens to their confessions, who confirms their children, who feeds them with the Bread of Life. It is the priest who holds up the ideal, who calls men to greatness, who steadies the hands of fathers as they raise their own children.

Here I want to be very clear that celibacy is a gift to the Church for a number of different reasons. Some of those reasons are practical. Their celibacy enables them to serve the needs of their community without the complicating factors of married life, as when a pastor can rise at 2:00 a.m. to visit a dying hospital patient without disturbing a family. While that is a gift, in my mind it is not the essential gift of the celibate, and certainly not the most valuable. After all, there are many married men who work professions involving long or irregular hours. Think, for example, of the doctor who frequently works night shifts at the hospital. No, in the case of a priest, it is not practical availability which is the most sacred fruit of celibacy; it is the spiritual and emotional fruitfulness that celibacy unlocks.

When a man, responding to the call of God, says yes to a celibate life, especially the life of a priest, he opens a channel in himself that is a source of life for others. This is nowhere more the case than a celibate man who indeed generates life for other fathers. In my own life experience, this has been nowhere more concretely illustrated than in my experience of the Sacrament of Confession. When I struggle with shame as a man — shame over my sin — it is Christ who forgives me. Full stop. Nevertheless, God in his abundance has ordained that I would have the opportunity to confess my sins to a priest in the context of confession.

Since becoming a married man, I have never been more grateful for the sacrament. On countless occasions I have found myself standing in a confession line, greeted by the compassionate eyes of a priest, confessing my sins, and being absolved. And while I also gain value from confessing my sins to my friends, there is something so breathtakingly beautiful about confessing them to a man who has devoted himself to the singular purpose of pastoring the Church and whose hands bear sacramental grace. I know that I am not placing a weight on this man by telling him things which, because of their gravity, might place an undue weight on his relationship with a wife and children. I know my secrets are secure with him. He stands in front of me as another Christ.

Yes, it's great that priests can be available at 2:00 a.m., but the gift of celibacy is much more than practicality. It is potently spiritually generative. It makes a difference. I have, on many occasions, sat in church as dozens of earthly fathers waited in line for a celibate man to hear their confessions. They came in shame. They left with hearts ablaze, equipped to return to their families and love their wives and their children. The priest had accompanied them from the garden of Gethsemane to the Resurrection garden. Quite truly, in part by virtue of his celibate love, whenever a priest sits in a confessional and channels God's forgiving grace, he reignites the masculine soul of the Church.

This is why the health of the priesthood is so essential to the health of fatherhood everywhere. When the priest is strong, when he is holy and masculine and full of grace, he strengthens the men around him. He models courage and self-mastery. He risks and he challenges. He protects. He generates.

I have concretely witnessed in many church communities that the manliness of the congregation mirrors that of the pastor. This should come as no surprise to masculine men, who naturally gravitate to men of like kind. But perhaps more substantially, the general mirroring that happens between pastors and congregations evidences a profound spiritual truth. Married couples give priests and nuns a concrete example of spousal gift, whereas priests and nuns remind married couples what their marriage is all about. The two vocations — marriage and priesthood — are mutually illuminating.

What does that mean? Consider a priest who is struggling to remember what God's love is like. He might wonder, "God, what is your love like? I gave up everything for you, but I don't understand you!" All this priest must do is look at a married couple in love, and it is as though God is saying to him, "My love for you is like that!" And the same is true for marriage. No marriage is perfect, and we can never find our complete fulfillment in another person. Priests and consecrated religious, male and female, are there to remind us that, in the end, it's not about our earthly marriages. The whole point of an earthly marriage is to point us towards the heavenly marriage, which the celibate person witnesses to every day. In this way, the two vocations shed light on each other. Married couples give a concrete witness. Celibate persons give a transcendent witness.[2]

What is true for the relationship between marriage and celibacy at large is also true specifically for the relationship between celibate men and their married brothers. When I, as a married man, see a priest who lives his spiritual fatherhood well, I am edified as a husband and father. In a good priest, I see a lived witness to the relationship between Christ and his Church, which of course is the very same witness that I am to give to my wife and children. I am deeply positively affected by masculine pastors. For this reason alone, the Catholic priesthood should not be regarded as less masculine; on the contrary, the priesthood is perhaps the most spiritually generative channel of the entire Church. Masculine priests are atomic bombs which explode grace into the lives of their congregations.

If we want strong families, we need strong fathers. But if we want strong fathers, we need strong priests — men who are not only icons of Christ, but who remind other icons what they are meant to be. The priest is not a spiritual bureaucrat. He is a patriarch of patriarchs. A father of fathers. A man whose celibate love ignites the masculine soul of the Church.

Heroic Celibates — Sacred and Lay

While the priesthood reveals celibacy in its most sacramental form, it is not the only arena in which celibate men demonstrate heroic masculinity. There are men — both religious and lay — who, by their chaste self-offering, have become radiant examples of strength, sacrifice, and spiritual generativity. These men are not defined by what they lack, but by what they give. They are celibate, not by accident or delay, but by vocation. And their impact has been seismic.

Consider St. Maximilian Kolbe. He was a Franciscan priest, celibate by vow, and entirely given over to the mission of evangelization and devotion to the Blessed Virgin Mary. But his most defining moment came in the brutality of Auschwitz. When Nazi guards selected ten men to die by starvation in reprisal for an escape, one of them, a husband and father, cried out in grief for his family. Kolbe stepped forward. "I am a Catholic priest," he said. "Let me take his place."

They let him. He died in that father's stead.

That moment has been remembered as one of the greatest modern acts of Christian sacrifice. But we must not overlook what made it possible. Kolbe could offer his life precisely because he had already given it. His celibacy, far from rendering him rootless or unmoored, had anchored him in Christ. He had trained his body and soul in the art of self-gift. And when the ultimate test came, he did not hesitate. His celibacy didn't make him passive. It made him available. It made him dangerous to evil. It made him free to protect a biological father.

That is generative masculinity.

St. Pier Giorgio Frassati, canonized by the Catholic Church in 2025, provides us with a different kind of example. A young Italian man from a wealthy family, Pier Giorgio never married. But he didn't postpone his mission while waiting for a spouse. He served the poor, climbed mountains, read philosophy, and prayed the Rosary daily. He brought his friends to Mass and gave his clothes to beggars. He was a force of joyful energy, a man utterly spent for the kingdom. And he did it all with an unencumbered freedom that only celibacy can offer.

Frassati's days were full — not with distraction, but with mission. He was involved in Catholic student groups, political activism, Eucharistic adoration, and service to the poor. He wrote letters to friends challenging them toward holiness and showed up with laughter and generosity wherever he went. Because he was unmarried, he had an unusual kind of availability — he could be everywhere, seemingly all at once.

And there are many men like Frassati today. Some are consecrated religious, others are confirmed singles, and still others are men single for a season. These men often mentor younger men who lack fathers, and just as often, they mentor those who do have fathers but need reinforcement in areas they aren't ready to share with their dads. These men buy plane tickets on a moment's notice to support a friend across the country. They lead missions. They serve on boards. They fill the gaps and enter the nooks and crannies of society that are difficult — sometimes impossible — for married men to occupy.

Whether permanently single or single for a time, these men have a unique gift to give. If you are in a season of singleness, don't waste it. Savor it. You have something now that you will never quite possess again, at least not in this same form. Marriage, if you are called to it, will be a great and glorious thing. But you will never again have the full freedom you possess today. This is the time to give boldly, to risk big, to love deeply. The unmarried years are not merely preparatory — they are missionary.

In Kolbe and Frassati we see a pattern emerge: celibate men who, though unmarried, are deeply fruitful. Their lives were not defined by isolation but by creative communion.

There is a kind of masculine strength exhibited only by men free of attachments. These men have the freedom to move swiftly toward need, to suffer in solidarity with strangers, to love without earthly ties. Every state of life lets the beauty of masculinity shine in its own color. The holiness of a husband will not look identical to that of a priest, a high school student, or a confirmed single man. But though the hues may differ, the light of the *Imago Dei* runs common in all contexts. Holy masculinity is a divine creation, regardless of the context in which it thrives.

This is why single men, whether priests, religious, or lay, deserve esteem and attention. When lived in virtue, their lives become wells of grace for the communities around them. They take on spiritual fatherhood, mentoring younger men, supporting parishes, organizing service, and stepping in where others cannot. And while many may never be canonized, their lives echo the pattern of saints: They generate life not by multiplying children, but by multiplying holiness. The Church needs these men. The world needs these men. And their witness stands as proof that masculinity is not diminished by celibacy — it is magnified by it.

When Celibacy Fails: The Anti-Icon

Of course, not every man who embraces celibacy lives it heroically. And not every priest or consecrated man has become a channel of spiritual life. We would be dishonest — and worse, we would be complicit — if we failed to acknowledge that celibacy, when corrupted, becomes not a sign of the kingdom but a scandal to it.

There is no wound in the modern Church so deep as the priestly abuse crisis. The horror of what was done to children, to the vulnerable, and to the trust of the faithful cannot be overstated. It is a crisis not only of sin, but of symbol. Celibacy, which is meant to be a radiant icon of Christ's total gift to the Church, becomes in such cases an anti-icon — a defaced image that repels rather than attracts.

Every priest sins. But grave betrayal from a man who is meant to stand *in persona Christi* shakes the soul of the Church. It is not only that evil has been done, but that a sacred space has been desecrated. When celibacy is not lived as a gift, it becomes a burden. When it is not supported by fraternity, prayer, and formation, it warps under pressure. When it is reduced to mere functional discipline — something a man tolerates for the sake of his job — rather than embraced as a path to spiritual fatherhood, it dries up. A man who is celibate but not generative, set apart but not poured out, is a contradiction in terms. And yet even here, the very scandal reaffirms the beauty of the vocation. Why is it so devastating when a priest fails? Because we know what he was meant to be. Because our hearts ache for the strength and holiness we expect to see in him. Because when celibacy is lived well, it changes the world.

The answer to corrupted celibacy is not to discard it. The answer is to call men to live it rightly. To prepare them, support them, and challenge them. To form priests who are truly fathers — men of prayer, discipline, humility, and courage. Men who stand at the altar with clean hands and full hearts. Men who make spiritual war for the sake of their people.

In short, we do not need fewer celibates. We need better ones. And we need the Church — especially her bishops and formators — to demand nothing less than heroic virtue from the men they ordain. From what I see of the young priests coming out of seminaries today, I am wildly excited for the future of the priesthood.

Men for the Kingdom

If there is one place in the Church today that most urgently needs a resurgence of authentic masculinity, it is at the highest levels of Church leadership. We need men, real men, at the altar. Men who are not afraid to lead, not afraid to speak hard truths, and not afraid to sacrifice.

The priest, for example, is not just a spiritual technician. He is not a sacramental functionary or a facilitator of community activities. He is the head of a family. And just as every family needs a strong father, every parish needs a strong priest — a man who governs with prudence, loves with tenderness, and protects with fierce resolve. We need men who can cultivate the garden of their spiritual community, protect it from serpents, and love it as a bride.

In the same way that families suffer at the hands of an effeminate man, so too do parishes suffer from effeminate pastors. Too often, our parishes suffer from a crisis of courage, a lack of willingness to take risks, and a lack of attention to the figurative garden of the parish community. In these instances, Church communities look more like overgrown weed beds rather than cultivated, fruitful gardens. This happens, for example, when a vocal minority dominates the tone of a parish, and the priest, unsure of how to respond, pulls back. It happens when Church programs drift from orthodoxy because a parish priest is too afraid to put the right people in leadership. It happens when priests, who should be trained to defend their flock from the lies of the culture, allow the secular culture to stride unchecked through the church door. Programs drift. Doctrine is softened. Secular culture creeps in. But a masculine priest doesn't allow that. He loves his flock enough to say no. He affirms his spiritual children just as Adam affirmed Eve. He protects his people from spiritual poison. He makes hard calls and sees them through. He does this not from a machismo authoritarianism, but out of fatherly love.

We don't need machismo pastors. We don't need clerical swagger. We do need priests who carry themselves with strength and stability. Men who can absorb conflict without crumbling, who can pray deeply and act decisively, who are courageous enough to be gentle and strong enough to say no. We need men who will not let the wolves inside the sheepfold.

When a father rises to the level of a true man, others rise with him — his wife, his children, his friends. But when a priest becomes a man, entire communities awaken. He becomes a spiritual patriarch, a father of fathers, a leader of families. His presence radiates order, peace, conviction. He reminds men who they are. And I will say it again: He reignites the masculine soul of the Church. And that's what we need.

Do not pursue the priesthood if you are not called. But if you are — if the Lord is calling you — then for the love of God and the Church, do not say no. The world does not need more hesitant men. It needs courageous ones. It needs priests who are bold enough to offer their strength and tender enough to offer their hearts. It needs spiritual fathers who know how to plant, prune, and protect — who can cultivate the garden of God with clarity and love.

And if God has not called you to the priesthood, but to serve the Church as a single man, then I want to speak to you directly: I need you. My children need you. This world needs you. The Church needs you. There are corners of the garden that I will never reach as a married man — places your presence can sanctify and transform. Mentor my sons. Encourage my daughters. Step into the breaches left open by absent fathers and overwhelmed families. Let your friendship be a source of grace. If the Lord is calling you to offer your singleness as a gift — whether for a season or for a lifetime — then lean into it. Say yes. The Church will be richer for it.

CHAPTER 7

Carving Pathways Forward

Since starting in men's outreach, I have had the privilege of collaborating with hundreds of Christian speakers, authors, and leaders. Whenever a man is scheduled to speak at one of our events, the standard practice is to ask for a brief biography. These bios are meant to give the audience a sense of who the speaker is and why he should be taken seriously.

Oftentimes the bios read something like this:

> *Frank McDonald was born in Chicago, Illinois. He graduated high school as valedictorian and then attended Princeton University, where he completed his undergraduate, master's, and PhD in five years. After Princeton, Frank joined the U.S. Navy and quickly ascended to commander of SEAL Team 6. Frank is known for dismantling*

> *an international terrorist network for which he received the Congressional Medal of Honor. After concluding his military service, Frank assumed leadership of a Fortune 500 company, authored multiple* New York Times *best-sellers, and composed five award-winning symphonies. Frank resides in New York with his wife and children.*

It's the subtlety of that last line that sticks with me. It may be just a sliver of the bio, but to me, a man's credibility hangs on how he lives that sliver.

I've never had the occasion to introduce my own dad in a public talk, but if I did, I suspect my introduction would be very short. It might sound like this: *This is Bo Bishop. He is an exceptional husband and a father.*

That's it. No degrees, no medals, no corporate accolades. Just two titles. The way my dad lives those titles is what makes him one of my heroes.

My favorite depiction of masculinity in film is in the character of Guido Orefice, the main character in the 1997 Italian film *Life Is Beautiful.* Guido is an incessantly optimistic man who falls hopelessly in love with Dora, marries her, and has a son, Giosuè. But Guido is also a Jew living under Nazi occupation. The most touching moments of the film portray a man who, even while hunted by the Nazis, steals time to romance his wife and delight his child. When Guido and Giosuè are confined to a concentration camp, he manages to convince his son that the camp is nothing more than a grand game of make-believe. Under the shadow of Nazi rifles, Guido spins stories, invents rules, and turns survival into play. In this way, he leads his family in a kind of dance through the war zone, where joy refuses to be extinguished despite the ever-present peril.

In many ways, my dad was like Guido. Guido knew the world was in trouble — he was under no illusions about that.

Likewise, most Christian men today know that the world is deeply confused. My dad carried that awareness, yet like Guido, he wove through the wreckage while keeping the laughter alive. He was shrewd when our family needed strength, and silly when his kids needed joy. Both mattered. Together, they formed a picture of manhood both steady and playful — strong enough to face the world's brokenness, yet lighthearted enough to make life beautiful.

My dad isn't perfect. But the way he lives is a testament to the quiet heroism found in any man who dares to lead a Christian family in today's fallen world. He took criticism with strength and levity. He endured financial and emotional hardship with grace. When the culture pulled his kids down a sinful road, he built a counterculture. Time and again, my parents made decisions that showed their family mattered more than any other earthly good. I will never forget, for example, when my dad — a popular hometown boy from Tampa, Florida — left it all behind to move our family to Des Moines, Iowa. The reasons were unique to our circumstances, but when my parents sensed it was best for us, they did it. Dad worked hard and was often recognized for his professional excellence. At times he put in long hours, but I never doubted that he would rather be at home than in the office.

There are a lot of great things that I could tell you about my dad. Among the things Dad did right, there are two that I want to highlight. The first is this: I never had even the slightest doubt that anything in his life mattered more than his relationship with my mom and with us, his children. Dad was not a genius, billionaire, or celebrity, but we were (and are) the center of his world. He now takes the same approach with his grandchildren.

The second is this: My dad had (and has) great friends. He didn't try to lead his family alone. He welcomed me into a community of men who were loyal, grounded, and faithful.

Growing up, I didn't see my dad as a man in isolation — I saw him as part of a community of men. The caricature biography of "Frank McDonald" above is, admittedly, a bit over the top. It sketches the outline of a kind of one-man army. In reality, no man fits that description, and wise men know it. My dad knew it, so he surrounded himself with a true army of friends, colleagues, and family.

I don't want to dress this up. If you had seen my dad fifteen years ago, in the thick of raising his family, at first glance you might not have thought there was anything remarkable about him or his friends. What set them apart was their intentionality. They methodically raised their kids within a community that celebrated God's design for men, women, marriage, and family. They created a vibrant, smart, attractive subculture that celebrated authentic masculinity and femininity. Each of my dad's friends brought a different shade of masculinity to the table: There were athletic men and musicians, businessmen and craftsmen, big personalities and introverts. Together, they painted a composite picture of masculinity: a rich, multi-dimensional vision of what it means to live as a man.

My father himself did not always have the same picture of manhood that he does today. He stepped into faith as an adult, joining a church for the first time in his twenties. Within that church he found an intentional, intergenerational community of men that taught him how to be a better man and eventually welcomed his sons into the same fellowship.

In a subtle way, my dad's life offers a blueprint for the way forward. Today's world is no longer Eden — it is a warzone. From sexuality and family life to the workplace and the classroom, the battle rages on every front, with the family at the center. Men are currently the weak point of the Christian family, and the project of the next generation is to restore them as the cornerstone. Great men are made in community. Whether you want to become a great man or raise one, you must throw your weight into building authentic, masculine, Christian communities. In this closing chapter, I want to outline the specific challenges that confront today's men and show why such communities are indispensable.

Today's Garden

Adam started as a man confident in his garden and in his relationship with Eve. Unfortunately, when sin entered the picture, Adam's entire world shifted beneath his feet. He felt ashamed before his woman. He felt estranged from the world, so he hid himself.

What happened to Adam happens still. The modern man has withdrawn from the family, the workplace, and the Church. Why? Here, it is worth recalling a foundational concept from our opening chapter: masculine fragility. Sociologists have long observed that the male sense of masculinity is more tenuous, more easily shaken, than its female counterpart. Men have an innate need to be affirmed not just as people, but as men.

Masculine fragility describes a kind of insecurity that arises when manhood feels unstable or easily threatened, leading to overreaction anger, withdrawal, posturing, or dismissiveness. Some critics use the term pejoratively, but it can also be analyzed more constructively: Fragile masculinity isn't just about ego — it's a symptom of men not having been initiated into a secure, positive vision of manhood.

Looking for male affirmation, young men naturally gravitate toward environments they perceive as masculine — places where they believe they might be affirmed in their masculinity. This reality implies that a healthy culture must ensure that its most fundamental institutions — family, workplace, school, and church — are genuinely affirming of masculine men. That is, they must be spaces where men feel they belong, where their strengths are called forth, and where they can flourish. Though there is some hope that the tide is beginning to turn, that is not what we see in today's culture, which accounts for the general male distancing from family, education, and religion.

Let's start with the family. The chief disruptor of the modern family life is the seismic shift in the sexual dynamics of our culture. For generations, American culture has fed young men a distorted script for sexuality, which glorifies conquest and celebrates license. We tell boys that sex has no real meaning, and they form their habits accordingly. But habits forged in adolescence die slowly. By the time those boys become husbands and fathers, the same patterns resurface, corroding families from within. Passion, which once called men upward toward greatness, is now twisted into a source of confusion and shame.

Where did this confusion begin — and where do we go from here? The modern sexual landscape shifted dramatically with the arrival of widespread contraception. Prior to 1930, no Christian denomination permitted its use. Then the Anglican Church broke with historic teaching and allowed contraception in certain cases. Within decades, nearly every denomination followed suit, quickly allowing its use in all circumstances. And though the Catholic Church itself never wavered, most American Catholics disobeyed Church teaching on this issue. By the 1970s, most American families were contracepting, and the sexual revolution was in full swing. For the first time in human history, the intrinsic bond between sex and children was severed, opening the way to an entirely new sexual ethic — or to no ethic at all.[1]

I say this with a heavy heart: Contraception has not helped the American family. It has hurt families. One of its consequences has been the creation of a sexual world that is fatally confusing for men. It has destabilized the sexual order and led, eventually, to the decline of fatherhood. Here my argument isn't primarily theological; it's biological.

I have never seen the point more elegantly stated than in the writings of evolutionary sociologist, Dr. Lionel Tiger of Rutgers University. Tiger makes a powerful yet disarmingly simple point about the modern male and his involvement in reproduction: For the first time since the dawn of the human race, the intrinsic connection between sexual relations and fertility has been drastically altered. What was once seen as a biological staple, the connection between sex and babies, is now fundamentally different. Contraception has changed the game. Further, the rules of the new game are unfairly weighted. It used to be the case that both sexes were on somewhat equal footing in their ability to predict whether a certain sexual act would result in pregnancy. Now, exactly the opposite is the case. Since the advent of modern contraception, virtually all the knowledge, responsibility, and power in the reproductive process lies in the hands of women.

Today's sexual landscape divests men from an adequate stake in the means of reproduction. The sexual seismic shift which began with contraception is now amplified by abortion laws which usually do not even require paternal notification (much less consent). Commenting about an unborn child in a 2019 stand-up routine, Dave Chappelle quipped, "If you can kill this motherf—er, I can at least abandon him. It's my money, my choice."[2]

The joke might be dark, but it finds resonance in the ears of the modern male. In the face of such a twisted moral situation, what do men do? Men walk. Figuratively and literally, they walk out on the family. They check out. Since 1960, the rate of fatherlessness in the United States has risen from 9% to 25%, and less than half of American kids reach adulthood with a biological father in the home.[3]

And when men walk, where do they go? They go to the places where something they are deeply wired for — sexuality — is now available at a cheaper price than ever before. The rise of high-speed internet pornography, online prostitution, and a host of other digital outlets has made counterfeit sexuality instantly accessible. Men are drawn to these hollow imitations because they are easy, available, and demand nothing in return. Meanwhile, committed sexual relationships — the kind that lead to fatherhood — have never been more fraught with danger. The combined effects of widespread contraception, legal abortion, and imbalanced custody laws have disincentivized men from pursuing lasting commitment. Put simply, no-strings-attached sex has never been easier to find, while genuine sexual intimacy has never carried a greater risk of peril.

I recognize that my critique of contraception may sound, to many readers, utterly out of step with modern life. For most people today, artificial birth control is as unremarkable as deodorant or toothpaste — simply part of the cultural wallpaper. Yet I must hold to what I see as plainly true: The widespread acceptance of contraception was the original toxin that fanned the sexual revolution into flame. That revolution has produced generations of sexual confusion, leading many men to disengage from family life.

In contrast to the cultural acceptance of contraception, many Christian families across denominations now embrace Natural Family Planning (NFP) or Fertility Awareness-Based Methods (FABMs) — scientifically advanced methods of achieving or avoiding pregnancy that cooperate with, rather than suppress, the God-given rhythms of a woman's body. This is a genuine sign of hope. To work in and through God's design is one thing, to work around it is another. The reverence this practice fosters toward sexuality naturally extends into a reverence for sexual difference itself — cultivating a deep respect for both masculinity and femininity.

You might think of sexuality as the mysterious heart of the human ecosystem. Ecosystems are delicate things. Contraception, or any other form of sexual sin, is like introducing a toxin into that ecosystem. Respect the integrity of the human ecosystem. Violating the ecosystem has and will continue to have negative consequences that we have only just begun to understand.[4]

Far be it from me to judge any person under the influence of our sexually confused culture. When the sexual revolution began, few could have foreseen its devastating cultural effects. And accepting things like contraception seem, on first blush, to be entirely harmless. But now that the sexual revolution has been established, we can judge it by its fruit. The fruit is bitter. It is time to uproot the tree. What once promised liberation has instead poisoned families and corroded the bond between men and women. For my part, I call for a full-scale return to timeless Christian teaching on sexuality. This means rejecting every counterfeit, from pornography and the collegiate hook-up culture to contraception itself. Only by recovering reverence for God's design of sexuality itself can we recover reverence for both masculinity and femininity.

What is true of the family is also, to a lesser degree, also true of the school system. Many books have been penned chronicling male educational decline. By this point the disparity is so stark that it has almost become a trope: "Girls do well in school and boys do not." In early years, the differences in male/female educational performance are more notable than differences that track across race and income. This, of course, is quite notable since enormous numbers of tax dollars each year are allotted to ameliorate other disparities, but relatively little to help boys in education. These disparities continue through to the university level. Bestselling author Dr. Leonard Sax, who has been following these stats for decades, recounts, "Over the last five decades, college campuses have undergone a sex change: they've changed from majority male to majority female." Here are the numbers from 1970 to 2025:

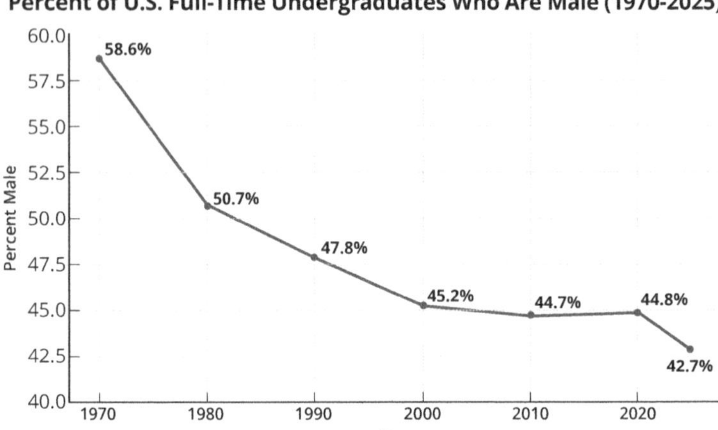

This crisis isn't new. As early as the 2000s, scholars like Sax and evolutionary biologist David Geary were sounding the alarm about boys falling behind in school. Two decades later, their warnings have become reality. Richard Reeves, in his book *Of Boys and Men*, shows that boys now lag behind girls in nearly every measure of academic achievement: They get lower grades, are less likely to graduate high school, and are far less likely to attend or finish college. The Center for Social Justice's 2025 *Lost Boys* report confirms this grim trajectory, warning of a "boyhood crisis" where male students are increasingly disengaged, underperforming, and dropping out of school systems that are ill-suited to their developmental needs. In reading, writing, and behavioral assessments, boys consistently trail girls by significant margins, setting them on a path of diminished opportunity before adulthood even begins. The data is clear: The male educational collapse is not coming — it's here, and it has been here for a while.[5]

Some may not find current university trends particularly troubling. After all, with a shortage of skilled workers in the trades and the burden of skyrocketing student loans, isn't it reasonable that fewer men and women are choosing to attend college? I'm quite sympathetic to that perspective. Still, I offer these statistics as evidence that many boys now view academics as a threat to masculine identity — yet another sphere where they're expected to check their man card at the door. Many schools today leave young boys feeling like imposters in what has become, in practice, a predominantly feminine environment. Like Adam in the garden after the fall, a space where boys once thrived has turned into a place of friction and unease. The workplace tells a slightly different story, but there are shared threads. Like the classroom, today's economy often leaves men with a lingering sense of displacement.

For most of human history, productive life was sharply divided by sex. Men hunted, fought, and undertook dangerous labor that turned risk into provision for others. In today's service economy, those tasks are now automated, recreational, or disdained, leaving "Man the Hunter," to borrow Lionel Tiger's phrase, largely unemployable. The loss is more than economic; it erases a traditional avenue for masculine altruism. As Roy Baumeister observes, men are unusually willing to endanger themselves for the sake of family and community, and it was in high-risk roles — soldier, builder, miner — that this impulse found noble expression. But in the contemporary economy, priority goes to the cubicle, not the barracks, and with this change a channel for masculine passion has been lost.[6]

At the risk of being misunderstood, let me be clear: I have had the privilege of working alongside exceptional female colleagues and leaders, to whom I am deeply indebted. I believe the modern workplace has been enriched by the contributions of women. I wholeheartedly encourage parents to raise daughters who are confident and capable in professional, extra-domestic settings. My point is not that women should remain confined to the home. Rather, it is that the workplace — once a primary outlet for masculine energy and purpose — has become less so. Many men have been displaced, and the rising rates of male joblessness suggest that a significant number are struggling to find their place in this new economic landscape.

One of the more troubling consequences of this cultural shift is that many men feel they have lost their sacred and distinctive role as providers.[7] Adam cultivated the garden for the sake of Eve, and throughout history, men have taken unparalleled pride in providing for those they love. In today's economy, however, where professionally capable and high-achieving women rightly excel, many men find themselves feeling sidelined — once again perceived as unnecessary. Even if a woman is unable to provide for her child, the state stands ready to intervene. Men are further displaced from a role in which they previously took great pride. Speaking to this trend, a men's sociologist recently made the chilling observation that "A remarkable new family pattern has emerged. I call it bureaugamy. A new trinity: a woman, a child, and a bureaucrat. Not monogamy. Not polygamy. Bureaugamy."[8]

The insecurity that arises when a man loses confidence in his work is profound. Studies show it is a substantially more jarring experience for men than for women.[9] A man who feels competent in his craft walks with a certain steadiness; he knows his place in the world. But when his work falters — when he feels unskilled, unneeded, or replaceable — his very sense of self begins to unravel. For most men, the collapse of confidence in their labor bleeds quickly into doubt about their strength, their value, even their masculinity itself.

Thus far I have shown that the garden of today's world has become a confusing place for men. Family, education, and work are markedly different for today's man than his historical predecessors. The places where they once found clear direction and meaning are now fraught with confusion. The only domain of public life we have not yet spoken about is the Church. In Chapter 5, we spoke about the reality of a female-dominated Church. But — at the risk of being prematurely optimistic — I want to highlight a potential bright spot emerging in the data.

For the first time in several generations, there are signs that young men may be turning back toward faith. According to recent reports from *The Economist* and the American Enterprise Institute, Generation Z is showing a surprising uptick in religious engagement, and much of it is being driven by young men. Among Gen Z born 2000–2006 the proportion identifying as Christian rose from 45% to 51% between 2023 and 2025. We already saw in Chapter 1 that, for the first time in decades, young men are now attending religious services more regularly than their female counterparts — a striking reversal of long-standing trends. *Axios* has likewise reported that weekly church attendance among Gen Z men has surpassed that of both millennials and Gen X men, signaling a possible revival of male religious engagement.[10]

Perhaps, after years of drifting in the cultural wilderness, young men are finally saying, "Enough is enough." Displaced from the workplace, the home, and traditional social roles, they are beginning to seek the one institution uniquely designed by God to restore order: the Church. Unlike modern cultural scripts, the Church has never wavered in affirming the beauty of male and female complementarity. "Male and female he created them" is not just a verse from Genesis — it is a blueprint for human flourishing. If this spiritual resurgence takes hold, it could become the cornerstone of a wider renewal, not just for men, but for society itself. A generation of men re-anchored in faith might finally begin to rebuild what was lost.

Pathways Forward

In the wake of the industrial, digital, and sexual upheavals of the last 150 years, it's neither realistic nor desirable to expect masculinity to look exactly as it did in previous generations. And frankly, for reasons already articulated, I'm not sure I would want it to. Every period of human history is an opportunity to renew God's timeless design in all its splendor. That's why, despite the challenges, I believe this is an exciting time to be a man.

As we work to restore authentic masculinity, my sense is that the winning strategies will look less like nuclear strikes and more like guerrilla campaigns. Some of the problems which beset men have a rather straightforward solution. For example, the state of today's sexual atmosphere in the West is so obviously misguided that the solution is simple: The modern male should reject the lust of the culture. He should reclaim Christianity's timeless sexual framework by rejecting things like infidelity, pornography, divorce, contraception, and cohabitation. He should embrace marriage, children, and family. Those might be difficult things to do, but at least they are straightforward.

The challenges facing men outside the sphere of marriage and family are more complex. How do we address the fact that boys are falling behind in school? What policies, pedagogies, and tools best equip them to thrive? How do we reawaken men to meaningful work in a disorienting economy? How do we draw them back into the worship of God? None of these questions admit of quick fixes, but all are solvable. Across the country, churches, schools, and workplaces are experimenting — testing ideas, refining methods, and making real progress. The best of these efforts share a common conviction: Helping men does not harm women. This is no zero-sum contest. Masculinity and femininity are not competitors but complements. To strengthen one is always to strengthen the other.

The problems which beset men in the family, the school, the Church, and the workplace will not be solved tomorrow, and I would like to provide a few concrete solutions all communities should embrace as they battle through the coming decades.

1. Embrace the Value of Single-Sex Spaces

In a culture that often prizes co-ed inclusivity, single-sex communities are frequently viewed with suspicion — sometimes as chauvinistic, exclusionary, or outdated. And to be fair, in some cases, they are. But at their best, male-only spaces are not about exclusion; they are about formation. They provide safe contexts where men can process what we've previously referred to as male fragility. They are places where men can be affirmed as men, where they can face challenges unique to the male experience, and where, especially for the young, they can safely grow into mature manhood.

All-male spaces are often dismissed as relics of a culture that assumed male superiority. But that charge misses something essential. In many cases, separating boys from girls — or men from women — is not about exclusion but about acknowledging real differences in the ways they grow, bond, and mature.

Anyone who has stepped into a kindergarten classroom has seen the difference. Girls, on average, develop the ability to sit still, focus, and follow directions at earlier ages. Boys, by contrast, learn best through movement, play, and trial-and-error. Place them side by side, and boys can quickly appear deficient, when in reality they are simply developing on a different timetable. Without space to learn in their own way, boys risk discouragement before they have even begun.[11]

The same principle carries into the spiritual life. Many young women display an early intuitive maturity in prayer and emotional connection with God. Their male peers often take longer to arrive at similar depth. In mixed settings, boys may withdraw or check out, feeling unable to keep pace. But in single-sex spaces, freed from premature comparison, they can grow into the men God intends them to be.

And what is true of boys is also true of men. Adult men often need time with other men to open up, be vulnerable, and bond in ways that simply do not come as easily in the presence of women. Around men, they are more likely to admit weakness, confront failure, or share wounds without fear of being diminished. Male-only environments — whether in prayer, brotherhood, or labor — create a unique space where trust can be forged and character deepened.[12]

This is not about privileging boys over girls or men over women. It is about recognizing that masculinity and femininity flourish differently, and that when men are given the time and space to grow together, both sexes are strengthened. Boys become better men, and men become better brothers, husbands, fathers, and leaders — not in competition with women, but in complement to them. In a culture where men are more confused than ever before, the value of exclusively male spaces has only increased.

While there is a value to national and international men's organizations as they provide unity and resources otherwise not possible, you don't need a big organization to gather a group of boys for a retreat, a small group, or even a monthly campfire. I personally have been inspired by what seems to be a groundswell of new, organic, local groups for young boys. If you have a good group that is local, that is a great resource. Lean into it.

2. Create a Small Community of Missionally-Aligned Men

My dad spent decades intentionally cultivating friendships with other men. Those friendships were an indispensable part of his success as a man and as a father. Do you have a circle of good men around you? If the answer is no, now is the time to start building that circle.

There are at least two reasons why this is critical. First, you personally will not be the man that you can be unless you have a group of close male friends. There is no one-size-fits-all solution to growth in manhood, but any man who pursues virtue in isolation will have blind spots. Iron sharpens iron. You need men speaking into the unique circumstances of your life.

Second, for the dads, these communities will be vital for the formation of your own sons. Even if you do not yet have children, I want to emphatically encourage all single men to begin cultivating the friendships now that can support your family in the future. The men who knew me as a single man have a unique window into my individual strengths and weaknesses. That window gives them powerful insight into my marriage. There are things you will say to your son that he might brush off or forget — but if he hears the same truths echoed and embodied by your friends, those lessons sink deeper and last longer. Male formation requires reinforcement from a community.

Boys don't just need words — they need models. As I've emphasized throughout this book, boys must have a picture of manhood to imitate. Ideally, that picture is drawn largely from their father. But it never comes exclusively from their father. Masculinity looks a little different from boy to boy and man to man. If your son has a particular personality type — say, he's quieter, more artistic, or more analytical — do you have men in your life who model how to live that kind of temperament well, as a flourishing, masculine man? The more diverse the examples of authentic masculinity your son sees, the richer his path to manhood will be.

3. Paint a Picture of the End Goal

In generations past, men might have accepted allowing their culture to guide them to manhood. Today's man must be more intentional. Aristotle taught us to pursue the *telos* — the end, the purpose — of any endeavor. Centuries later, Stephen Covey echoed the same wisdom in simpler terms: "Begin with the end in mind." When it comes to forming men (either yourself or your sons), this is indispensable advice.

Several years ago, I sat down with a group of dads to walk through an exercise recommended by New York City pastor Jon Tyson — an exercise I believe has enormous value not only for fathers but also for any man seeking to be a better man.[13] It goes like this: Picture the day your son leaves home on his eighteenth birthday. Or, alternatively, picture yourself ten years from now. Then ask yourself a few simple but profound questions:

- What qualities do I want the man that I envision to possess?
- What do I want him to know?
- What do I want him to have experienced?

Take a few minutes to write down your answers. Then ask yourself a second set of questions:

- For dads: Do I personally possess the qualities I want my son to have? Do I know what I want him to know? Have I experienced what I want him to experience?
- For single men: Where do I fall short of the manhood I envision for myself? What qualities do I lack?

If this exercise seems challenging, that's normal, especially for dads. Having had conversations with hundreds of fathers, I've come to believe that many — if not most — men don't really get serious about becoming men until they have other souls entrusted to their care. Fatherhood makes a father of you.

Once you've recognized that, move to part two of the exercise: What concrete steps are you going to take over the next one, five, ten, and twenty years to build both yourself — and, if you're a dad, your son — into the man you hope he will become? Whatever plan you make, the experiences, conversations, and knowledge that you impart to your son will become his path of initiation into manhood, something he desperately needs. So take the plan seriously! It will likely change along the way; life has a way of adjusting our maps. But if you haven't at least sketched a route to the destination, you almost certainly won't get there.

Becoming the Picture

Since founding an organization devoted to fatherhood, I have traveled the country with a small production team, gathering the stories of men. I've listened to fathers who sacrificed sleep to provide, sons who leaned on a dad's quiet strength, and daughters who never forgot his tender care. These testimonies have left me humbled and grateful, a reminder that there are far more good men in the world than the headlines ever admit. After hearing hundreds of stories, it takes a lot to stop me in my tracks. But one story — told to me years ago by one of my wife's friends — still does.

She came from a large family in northern Virginia: the Vander Woudes. Her grandfather, Thomas, was a Vietnam veteran and a retired airline pilot. By 2008, most of his sons were grown, but his youngest, Joseph — "Josie" — was still at home. Josie was twenty years old and had Down syndrome. He and his dad were inseparable, companions in nearly everything. If you saw Tom, chances are you saw Josie too.

One warm September afternoon, Tom and his son Josie were working outside on their small farm. Josie wandered across the yard and stepped onto the brittle lid of an old septic tank. In an instant it collapsed, and he plunged seven feet down into a pit of sewage. The stench burned his lungs. Panic overtook Josie, and in the struggle he even swallowed some of the filth.

Tom sprang into action. He lunged to the opening and peered down. One look at the depth of the tank and the smell of toxic fumes told Tom that Josie didn't have long. He shouted to a workman nearby, urging him to tell Mary Ellen — his wife — to call 911. Then, without wasting a second, Tom swung his legs over the edge and dropped in himself.

Once inside the septic tank, Tom braced himself beneath Josie, trying to lift him toward the workman who was now pulling from above. The methane and other poisonous gases were overpowering; there was almost no fresh air to breathe. Gasping, Tom shouted, "You pull and I'll push!" With those final words, he wedged himself under Josie for one more attempt. The fumes overtook him, and Tom lost consciousness. Slipping beneath the surface, Tom's limp body still propped up his son.

When rescuers arrived, Josie was alive. Tom was not.

The image is searing: a father's final breath spent beneath the mire so his son might live. That act of love has inspired thousands — perhaps hundreds of thousands — first in northern Virginia and now throughout the country. Scenes like this grip the human imagination, stirring both our loftiest aspirations and our most primal desires. Bad men may have earned our culture's suspicion, but great men still command its awe. Thomas Vander Woude raised seven sons — exceptional men. One became a priest; several others are now leading strong families of their own.[14] His sons had a living picture of masculinity. They saw the love of God made flesh in the daily, embodied witness of their father.

So how do we make more men like Thomas Vander Woude? In these chapters I have argued for a renewed vision of masculine flourishing. What does it look like? It looks like Adam working the Garden and delighting in Eve. It looks like men who refuse to cave to shame, to the temptations to dominance, and distance, but instead surrender their shame to Christ in Gethsemane. It looks like men who, through grace, die to their sin and rise as New Adams in the garden of the Resurrection. It looks like fathers who become living icons of the Heavenly Father to their children, protecting and providing not only materially, but emotionally and spiritually.

This is the call. This is the theological picture. But theology alone does not transform a man. Men transform men. Renewal begins when the truth takes on flesh before our eyes. Thomas Vander Woude stirs us because he was a concrete person living in the same 21st-century world we inhabit.

Men need the picture in flesh and blood. Christ is that picture made perfect, but the world still needs to see it alive in you. So, embody it. Be the picture. Become an icon of the New Adam.

Notes

Chapter 1: Men Without a Map

1. For a thorough investigation into the cross-cultural reality of male rites of passage, see David D. Gilmore, *Manhood in the Making: Cultural Concepts of Masculinity* (Yale University Press, 1991), 220.

2. See Jean Garnett, "The Trouble With Wanting Men," *New York Times Magazine*, July 21, 2025, https://www.nytimes.com/2025/07/21/magazine/men-heterofatalism-dating-relationships.html.

3. Belinda Luscombe, "Why Women Are More Likely Than Men to Initiate Divorces," *Time*, August 21, 2015. Luscombe notes that "about two-thirds of all divorces are initiated by women, a figure that has held steady for decades."

4. Over the past three decades, the percentage of American men reporting six or more close friends fell from 55% to just 27%, while those with no close friends at all surged from 3% to 15% — evidence of what social scientists now call a "friendship recession." See Daniel A. Cox, "The State of American Friendship: Change, Challenges, and Loss," Survey Center on American Life, June 8, 2021, https://www.americansurveycenter.org/research/the-state-of-american-friendship-change-challenges-and-loss/.

5. Between 2000 and 2022, the age-adjusted suicide rate increased by ap-

proximately 35%, from around 17.7 per 100,000 for males in 2000 to a peak of 22.8 in 2018, and then again rising to around 22.9 in 2022. This trend reflects an overall 30–35% rise across the period, with the highest recorded rates since World War II. In 2022, the male suicide rate was approximately four times higher than the rate for females (22.9 vs. 5.9 per 100,000). These trends indicate both a substantial increase and a widening gender gap in suicide rates. For further investigation, see Matthew F. Garnett and Sally C. Curtin, "Suicide Mortality in the United States, 2001–2021," NCHS Data Brief, no. 464 (2023): https://www.cdc.gov/nchs/products/databriefs/db464.htm; Matthew F. Garnett and Sally C. Curtin, "Suicide Mortality in the United States, 2022," NCHS Data Brief, no. 509 (2024): https://www.cdc.gov/nchs/products/databriefs/db509.htm.

6. Though increases are not as drastic as in the second half of the twentieth century, the early part of the twentieth century has seen similar increases in cohabitation and divorce. Here these is hardly a need to cite evidence, but please see Jill Daugherty and Casey Copen, "Trends in Attitudes About Marriage, Childbearing, and Sexual Behavior: United States, 2002, 2006–2010, and 2011–2013," *Natl Health Stat Report* 92 (2016): 1–10, PMID: 27019117.

7. See, for example, Kerwin Kofi Charles and Ming Ching Luoh, "Male Incarceration, the Marriage Market, and Female Outcomes," *The Review of Economics and Statistics* 92, no. 3 (2010): 614–627. Here, in a manner consonant with other studies, the authors reference disproportionately high and disparately rising male incarceration rates. Further, they conclude with an interesting claim which further evidences the difficulties of the crisis of masculinity: "Higher male imprisonment appears to have lowered the likelihood that women marry, modestly reduced the quality of their spouses when they do marry, and shifted the gains from marriage away from women and toward men."

8. For a thorough-going chronicling of this shift, see Leonard Sax's *Boys Adrift*, a revised edition of which is set for release in 2026.

9. Roy F. Baumeister, *Is There Anything Good About Men?: How Cultures Flourish by Exploiting Men* (Oxford University Press, 2010). See also Roy F. Baumeister and Kathleen D. Vohs, "Sexual Economics, Culture, Men, and Modern Sexual Trends," *Society* 49, no. 6 (2012): 520–524.

10. See especially Warren Farrell, *The Myth of Male Power: Why Men Are the Disposable Sex* (Simon & Schuster, 1993).

11. Richard V. Reeves, *Of Boys and Men: Why the Modern Male Is Struggling, Why It Matters, and What to Do about It* (Brookings Institution Press, 2022).

12. In general, men are more likely than women to cheat: 20% of men and 13% of women reported that they've had sex with someone other than their spouse while married, according to data from the recent General Social Survey (GSS) 2010–2016.

13. See Curtis Silver, "Pornhub 2017 Year in Review Insights Report Reveals Statistical Proof We Love Porn," *Forbes*, January 9, 2018, https://www.forbes.com/sites/curtissilver/2018/01/09/pornhub-2017-year-in-review-insights-report-reveals-statistical-proof-we-love-porn/#eb2f0d024f55; Barna Group and Josh McDowell, *The Porn Phenomenon: The Impact of Pornography in the Digital Age* (Barna Group, 2016); Mary Eberstadt, *Adam and Eve After the Pill: Paradoxes of the Sexual Revolution* (Ignatius Press, 2012); Janet E. Smith, ed., *Why Humanae Vitae Is Still Right* (Ignatius Press, 2018).

14. See Maria Cancian et al., "Who Gets Custody Now? Dramatic Changes in Children's Living Arrangements After Divorce," *Demography* 51, no. 4 (2014): 1381–1396.

15. See Joseph Pleck, *The Myth of Masculinity* (MIT Press, 1983), 133.

16. Mary Eberstadt does an excellent job of chronicling the demise of Christian denominations that reject timeless Christian sexual teachings. See Mary Eberstadt, *Adam and Eve After the Pill, Revisited* (Ignatius Press, 2023), 125–141.

17. For example, there is a growing movement within contemporary psychology to extol positive images of masculinity as a solution to the crisis. Those interested in this movement may start by looking at Ryon McDermott's work on the Positive Psychology Positive Masculinity Paradigm.

18. See guidelines here: https://www.apa.org/about/policy/boys-men-practice-guidelines.pdf.

19. Brian P. Cole, "*Psychology of Men and Masculinities'* Focus on Positive Aspects of Men's Functioning: A Content Analysis and Call to Action," *Psychology of Men and Masculinities* 22, no. 1 (2021): 39–47.

20. Concepts related to what this book calls masculine fragility have received a great deal of interest in the last two decades of psychological research. For those interested in more literature on this point, the "Precarious Manhood Thesis" argues that manhood is fundamentally "precarious" or fragile insofar as it is "both difficult to achieve and tenuously held." As the study "Hard Won and Easily Lost" shows: "Compared with womanhood, which is typically viewed as resulting from a natural, permanent, and biological developmental transition, manhood must be earned and maintained through publicly verifiable actions." Joseph A. Vandello and Jennifer Bosson, "Hard Won and Easily Lost: A Review and Synthesis of Theory and Research

on Precarious Manhood," *Psychology of Men and Masculinity* 14, no. 2 (2013): 101–113.

21. For these and other statistics illustrating the gravity of fatherhood declines, see the National Fatherhood Initiative (www.fatherhood.org). See also "Current Population Survey, 2006 Annual Social and Economic (ASEC) Supplement," United States Bureau of the Census, archived March 4, 2013, at https://web.archive.org/web/20130304014610/http://www.census.gov/apsd/techdoc/cps/cpsmar06.pdf.

22. Survey Center on American Life. 2023. *Survey on Religious Disaffiliation among Generation Z.* American Enterprise Institute, April. Report, Survey Center on American Life. Washington, DC.

Chapter 2: Man in Eden

1. "Profile of Women and Gender Studies Departments," American Academy of Arts and Sciences, Fall 2017.

2. *Catechism of the Catholic Church*, par. 1703.

3. John Paul II, *Letter to Women* (Pauline Books & Media, 1995), par. 7.

4. A close reading of the second creation account does indeed reveal a sequential creation of man and woman. The text shows that the substance from which the woman, Eve, is created is that of the male, Adam. Genesis clearly indicates a sequential creation of man followed by woman. Genesis 2:22–23 states that the matter from which the woman (*'ishshah*) is formed is from the *ha-'adam* and that the woman (*'ishshah*) was taken out of the *'ish*. The corresponding passages in Genesis read as follows: "And the Lord God fashioned into a woman [*'ishshah*] the rib which He had taken from the man [*ha-'adam*], and brought her to the man [*ha-'adam*]. And the man [*ha-'adam*] said, "This is now bone of my bones, / And flesh of my flesh; / She shall be called Woman [*'ishshah*], / Because she was taken out of Man [*'ish*]." The *ha-'adam*, from whom the rib was taken, is identified as the *'ish* from whom the woman (*'ishshah*) was taken. Though the Hebrew *ha-'adam* in Genesis 2 is oftentimes used as a collective concept referring to the entire human species, the Genesis text is clear; the woman (*'ishshah*) is created from a male substance (*'ish*). The use of *ha-'adam* to refer to "man" in this passage leads to the conclusion that the *ha-'adam* is a reference to a specific "human being," in this case a man. In the Hebrew, *'adam* without the definitive article *ha*, can refer to man in the collective sense. But when the definitive article is used, it is a reference to a specific "human being," and, in this case, according to the narrative that follows, one who is male. Thanks to Dr. Joseph Atkinson for assistance

with the exegesis on this point. I would also like to note that while Adam is created prior to Eve, one can still make observations about Adam which apply to both sexes, something John Paul II does in his Theology of the Body.

5. Simon Baron-Cohen, *The Essential Difference: Men, Women and the Extreme Male Brain* (Basic Books, 2003).

6. Dr. Gregory Bottaro, "On the Masculine Genius," *Humanum Review* 8, no. 2 (2018): 29–34. See also Katherine Keller and Vinod Menon, "Gender Differences in the Functional and Structural Neuroanatomy of Mathematical Cognition," *Neuroimage* 47, no. 1 (2009): 342–52.

7. Enuma Elish, Tablet II, lines 105–110, and Tablet VI, lines 1–8, in *Ancient Near Eastern Texts Relating to the Old Testament*, ed. James B. Pritchard, trans. E. A. Speiser (Princeton University Press, 1969), 66, 72. For a broader discussion of Babylonian creation myths and their theological contrast with Genesis, see Lawrence Boadt, *Reading the Old Testament: An Introduction* (Paulist Press, 2012), 111–118.

8. Baumeister, *Is There Anything Good About Men*? 64.

9. See Baumeister, Is There Anything Good About Men?, 79. I have always found the findings of evolutionary biology to be among the most illuminating observations of the human psyche. On this particular point, I am particularly indebted to sociologist and Jesuit priest Fr. Walter Ong. See also Walter J. Ong, *Fighting for Life*: *Contest*, *Sexuality*,' (Cornell University Press, 1981), 53. For more contemporary evidence supporting the evolutionary basis of male expendability, see David C. Geary, *Male*, *Female*: The Evolution of Human Sex Differences, 3rd ed. (American Psychological Association, 2021), especially chapters 4–6; and J. M. Plavcan, "Sexual dimorphism in primate evolution," *American Journal of Physical Anthropology* 116.S33 (2001): 25–53, which examines body size and competition as factors in male-male aggression and reproductive variance.

10. John Chrysostom, "Homilies on Genesis" 1–17, trans. Robert C. Hill, *The Fathers of the Church*, vol. 74 (Catholic University of America Press, 1986), 99.

11. John Chrysostom, "Homilies on Genesis," 109.

12. Augustine, "The Literal Meaning of Genesis," trans. John Hammond Taylor, vol. 1, *Ancient Christian Writers*, no. 41 (Newman Press, 1982), 391.

Chapter 3: Men in Sin

1. Ambrose, "Paradise", trans. Dennis K. Quinn, in *Saint Ambrose: Seven Exegetical Works, The Fathers of the Church*, vol. 65 (Catholic University of

America Press, 1972), 100. "Why did Adam not restrain her, when he saw she had been deceived? Why did he not ward off the serpent?" — Book I, ch. 7.

2. Ephrem the Syrian, *Hymns on Paradise*, trans. Sebastian Brock (St. Vladimir's Seminary Press, 1990), 88. "It was not fitting that she, who had heard the command secondhand, should confront the serpent alone." — Hymn 3.6.

3. John Chrysostom, "Homilies on Genesis," 220. "He ought to have stopped the woman and corrected her and reminded her of the commandment. Instead, he kept silent and took the fruit." — Homily 16.

4. Karol Wojtyła's *Love and Responsibility* is very helpful for understanding this point. Wojtyla says quite plainly that "Shame is a tendency, uniquely characteristic of the human person, to conceal sexual values sufficiently to prevent them from obscuring the value of the person as such." He goes on to say that the purpose of tendency is actually the "self-defense of the person." Understood in this sense, Wojtyla is careful to say that shame, in some of its manifestations, is actually a positive reaction. After all, a complete lack of shame (i.e., shamelessness) would be to concede to a denigration of the person, as, for example, in such impersonal sexual experiences as pornography. Unlike shamelessness, a positive experience of shame is not only a defense, but also an invitation to enter into the personal domain of a sexual experience. Eve's covering of herself is both a rejection of Adam's lustful glance and an invitation for him to reclaim the personal nature of his sexuality. As Wojtyla says, that shame has "a dual significance: it means flight, the endeavor to conceal sexual values so that they do not obscure the values of the person as such, but it also means the longing to inspire or experience love. ... Thus our analysis of sexual shame shows that it clears the way, so to speak, for love." In this manner, an appropriate understanding of shame is not a hindrance to love, but actually an enhancement of love insofar as it encourages love's personal dimension. Karol Wojtyła, *Love and Responsibility*, trans. H. T. Willetts (Ignatius Press, 1993), 182.

5. I have always thought Augustine's reflections on this theme in *City of God* get to the heart of the matter, highlighting the goodness of the body/humanity, but the shame over man's corrupted nature: "It is right, therefore, to be greatly ashamed of this lust, and it is right that the members which it moves or fails to move by its own right, so to speak, and not completely in accord with our will should be called shameful, which they were not called before man's sin. For, as it is written, 'And they were naked, and were not ashamed.' This was not because they did not know that they were naked; rather, their nakedness was not yet disgraceful, because lust did not yet

arouse those members independently of their will. The flesh did not yet give testimony, as it were, of man's disobedience by disobedience of its own." Augustine, *The City of God against the Pagans*, trans. R. W. Dyson (Cambridge University Press, 1998), 615. Emphasis mine. And later in book 17, "It was not the nudity of their bodies that made them ashamed, but the disorder of their passions. The fact that their flesh gave no response to their will was the proof and penalty of their rebellion against God's will."

6. The male proclivity toward dominance is evident to common sense, but it is also strongly supported by contemporary psychological literature. The leading textbook on men and masculinities frames the entire field of men's studies as an attempt to explore "versions of masculinity that do not dominate women." Few cultural moments underscored this need more forcefully than the #MeToo movement of 2018, which served as a searing public rebuke of dominant masculinity. Of all the criticisms aimed at traditional masculinity, perhaps none is more common — or more damning — than its tendency to establish unjust power over women. This theme is also well-documented in research on Gender Role Conflict (GRC), which consistently shows that men are more likely to assert an unjust form of dominance when under stress, particularly when they feel they are failing to meet societal standards of manhood. The modern concept of "toxic masculinity" is rooted almost entirely in this tendency toward dominance. If there is one trait most despised in men today, it is the unjust control and abuse of power they have historically exercised.

7. For a thoroughgoing, long-form presentation of this same argument, please see Baumeister, *Is There Anything Good About Men*?

8. Having worked with Joshua several times, I heartily recommend that any ministry leader engage him as a speaker and teacher. You can find out more about Joshua and contact his team here: https://www.joshuabroome.me/. His recent book is fantastic: *7 Lies That Will Ruin Your Life: What My Journey from Porn Star to Preacher Taught Me About the Truth That Sets Us Free* (FaithWords, 2024).

9. See Broome, *7 Lies That Will Ruin Your Life*, 188–192.

10. Broome, *7 Lies That Will Ruin Your Life*, 190.

11. Meg Meeker, *Strong Fathers, Strong Daughters: 10 Secrets Every Father Should Know* (Ballantine Books, 2012), 15.

12. The masculine tendency to distance oneself from intimacy in moments of ego-threat has strong grounding in both neuroscience and psychology. Louann Brizendine argues that male sensitivity to rank is rooted in evolutionary pressures of male–male competition, leaving men more pre-

occupied with hierarchical standing than with the relational quality of their bonds. She notes that in her counseling practice, the male stress response to workplace promotions and demotions consistently outstrips that of women, underscoring how deeply status-consciousness is tied to male self-worth. This helps explain why, when threatened, men often withdraw emotionally rather than engage vulnerably. Contemporary psychology has reached similar conclusions. From a young age, threats to masculine identity tend to produce displays of toughness and suppression of distress rather than relational openness. In one study, Stephen Fowler and Andrew Geers found that college men whose masculinity was questioned responded by demonstrating emotional stamina and an ability to withstand physical and emotional pain without showing distress. This corresponds to the wider literature documenting that when their masculinity is threatened, men often engage in emotional distancing as a protective strategy. Taken together, these findings suggest that male externality and detachment are not simply cultural accidents, but patterned responses with roots in evolutionary history and continuing confirmation in psychological research. See Louann Brizendine, *The Male Brain: A Breakthrough Understanding of How Men and Boys Think* (Broadway Books, 2010), 108–12; Stephanie L. Fowler and Andrew L. Geers, "Does trait masculinity relate to expressing toughness? The effects of masculinity threat and self-affirmation in college men," *Psychology of Men and Masculinity* 18, no. 2 (2017): 176–86.

13. The tradition that Satan fell by refusing to serve the Incarnate Christ — summarized in the phrase *non serviam* ("I will not serve") — has deep roots in Christian thought, though it is not explicitly found in Scripture. The phrase itself is drawn from Jeremiah 2:20, where rebellious Israel declares, "I will not serve." In later tradition, especially among Latin theologians, this defiant cry is attributed to Lucifer as a way of expressing the pride and disobedience underlying the angelic fall. See *Biblia Sacra Vulgata*, ed. Robert Weber, 5th ed. (Deutsche Bibelgesellschaft, 2007), Jer 2:20. In the Franciscan theological tradition, the idea takes fuller shape. Saint Bonaventure suggests that the angels fell through pride at God's ordering of creation, which they found intolerable — an early hint at their rejection of a divine plan marked by humility. See Bonaventure, "Collationes in Hexaemeron," in *Opera Omnia*, vol. 5 (Collegium S. Bonaventurae, 1891), especially Coll. XIX, 15. Bl. John Duns Scotus later develops this further in his doctrine of the absolute primacy of Christ — the teaching that the Incarnation was part of God's eternal plan irrespective of the Fall. While Scotus does not say explicitly that the angels were shown the Virgin and refused to serve, his framework laid the

theological foundation for this view. On this, see John Duns Scotus, "Reportatio Parisiensis," in *Opera Omnia*, ed. C. Balić et al., vol. 20 (Typis Polyglottis Vaticanis, 2005), lib. III, dist. 7; Allan B. Wolter, *The Philosophical Theology of John Duns Scotus* (Purdue University Press, 1995), 135–38.

Chapter 4: New Adams

1. Victor Hugo, *Les Misérables*, trans. Charles E. Wilbour (Carleton, 1862), 85.

2. Ibid., 86.

3. Fulton J. Sheen, *Life of Christ* (McGraw-Hill, 1958), 336.

4. C. S. Lewis, *That Hideous Strength: A Modern Fairy-Tale for Grown-Ups*, (Scribner, 1996), chapter 15.

5. See Augustine, "Tractates on the Gospel of John," 112–124, trans. John W. Rettig, *The Fathers of the Church*, vol. 90 (Catholic University of America Press, 1995), tractate 116.

6. See John Chrysostom, "Homilies on the Gospel of St. John and the Epistle to the Hebrews," trans. Philip Schaff, *Nicene and Post-Nicene Fathers*, First Series, vol. 14, ed. Philip Schaff (Hendrickson, 1994), homily 83.

7. See John Paul II, *Redemptoris Custos* (Guardian of the Redeemer), (Libreria Editrice Vaticana, 1989). Throughout this text, particularly in §12, John Paul II likens Joseph's "yes" to the angel as parallel to Mary's annunciation.

8. Mary Stanford offers a particularly clear treatment of headship, presenting it not as a relic of repression but as a Christian ideal to be embraced and lived in the unique circumstances of each marriage. See Mary Stanford, *The Obedience Paradox: Finding True Freedom in Marriage* (Our Sunday Visitor, 2022).

9. Pope Pius XI, in his encyclical Casti Connubii (On Christian Marriage) affirms an inherent order of the family and stresses that this order will always remain a teaching of the Church. Pius XI's words are quite firm:

"Domestic society being confirmed, therefore, by this bond of love, there should flourish in it that 'order of love,' as St. Augustine calls it. This order includes both the primacy of the husband with regard to the wife and children, the ready subjection of the wife and her willing obedience, which the Apostle commends in these words: 'Let women be subject to their husbands as to the Lord, because the husband is the head of the wife, and Christ is the head of the Church'" (26). Now, it should be noted that the subjection referred to by Pope Pius excludes anything like slavery. He takes great care to note that the wife should be regarded as a "companion" and not a servant (27). He writes in paragraph 27: "This subjection, however, does not deny or take away the liberty which fully belongs to the woman both in view of her dignity as a human person, and in view of her most noble office as wife and mother and companion; nor does it bid her obey her husband's every request if not in harmony with right reason or with the dignity due to wife. ... But it forbids that exaggerated liberty which cares not for the good of the family; it forbids that in this body which is the family, the heart be separated from the head to the great detriment of the whole body and the proximate danger of ruin. For if the man is the head, the woman is the heart, and as he occupies the chief place in ruling, so she may and ought to claim for herself the chief place in love." Pius XI, *Casti Connubii* (On Christian Marriage), Vatican.va.

10. "Ancient Homily on Holy Saturday", in *The Liturgy of the Hours*, vol. 2 (Catholic Book Publishing, 1976), 496–497.

11. See Hippolytus of Rome, "Commentary on the Song of Songs," in *The Song of Songs: Interpreted by Early Christian and Medieval Commentators*, trans. and ed. Richard A. Norris Jr. (William B. Eerdmans Publishing Company, 2003), 71–72; Ambrose of Milan, *Exposition of the Holy Gospel According to Saint Luke*, trans. Theodosia Tomkinson (Center for Traditionalist Orthodox Studies, 1998).

12. See Augustine, *Tractates on the Gospel of John* 112–124, tractate 121.3, page 13.

13. See Gregory the Great, "Homilies on the Gospels 25.9," in *Forty Gospel Homilies*, trans. David Hurst, Cistercian Studies Series, vol. 123 (Cistercian Publications, 1990), 201.

Chapter 5: Dads and the Domestic Church

1. Gordon Zahn, *Solitary Witness: The Life and Death of Franz Jägerstätter* (Templegate Publishers, 1986).

2. See Vern L. Bengston et al., *Families and Faith: How Religion is Passed Down Across Generations* (Oxford University Press, 2017), 76-77.

3. "Nationwide Study on Faith and Relationships: Final Report," *Communio*, June 2023, https://communio.org/faith-and-relationships-study.

4. "The Gender Gap in Religion Around the World,' Pew Research Center, March 22, 2016, https://www.pewresearch.org/religion/2016/03/22/the-gender-gap-in-religion-around-the-world/.

5. "Religious Landscape Study: 2023–2024," Pew Research Center, Feb-

ruary 2025, https://www.pewresearch.org/religion/2025/02/26/decline-of-christianity-in-the-us-has-slowed-may-have-leveled-off/.

6. Ryan P. Burge, "Why Young Women Aren't More Religious Than Men Anymore," *Christianity Today*, July 2022, https://www.christianitytoday.com/2022/07/young-women-not-more-religious-than-men-gender-gap-gen-z.html.

7. I am forever indebted to Joseph Atkinson for many conversations on these and other points. His work on this topic is foundational to my understanding. To date, I think his book on the domestic church and the father's role in it is more theologically astute and accurate than anything else I have read on the topic. See Joseph C. Atkinson, *Biblical and Theological Foundations of the Family: The Domestic Church* (Catholic University of America Press, 2014), 78–90.

8. The Catholic tradition speaks of the family as the "domestic church" (CCC 1655–1658). Within this domestic church, parents — especially fathers — exercise a unique role of spiritual leadership. John Paul II writes in *Familiaris Consortio*: "In their role as parents, fathers and mothers receive the grace of the sacrament of Matrimony to educate their children in faith and in the Church. By virtue of this mission, they share in the priesthood of Christ, not by conferring sacraments, but by leading their children to God through witness, teaching, and prayer" (John Paul II, Familiaris Consortio, 38). Similarly, Pope Benedict XVI affirmed the father's priestly role in the home, stating: "Every home is a domestic church in which parents are the first heralds of the faith to their children. Fathers, especially, are called to exercise a priestly role in the family, teaching prayer, blessing their children, and guiding them in Christian formation" (Benedict XVI, "Address to the Plenary Assembly of the Pontifical Council for the Family," December 1, 2011, Vatican.va.)

9. See John Paul II, "Homily in Perth, Australia, November 30, 1986," Vatican.va.

10. Vern L. Bengston et al., *Families and Faith*, 71–98.

11. Ibid.

12. One of our interviewees, Dr. Leonard Sax, is particularly emphatic on this point. He cites both his own research and writings, particularly his 2017 book, *The Collapse of Parenting*, in which he argues that parents who neglect to discipline their children do their kids a disservice. See Leonard Sax, *The Collapse of Parenting: How We Hurt Our Kids When We Treat Them Like GrownUps* (Basic Books, 2017). For those interested in learning more about an authoritative style of parenting, I heartily encourage the work of Di-

ana Baumrind. Baumrind, a clinical and developmental psychologist, coined the following parenting styles: authoritative, authoritarian, and permissive/indulgent. Later, Maccoby and Martin added the uninvolved/neglectful style. See Diana Baumrind, "Authoritative Parenting Revisited: History and Current Status," in *Authoritative Parenting: Synthesizing Nurturance and Discipline for Optimal Child Development*, ed. Robert E. Larzelere, et al. (American Psychological Association, 2013).

13. Don Everts, T*he Spiritually Vibrant Home: The Power of Messy Prayers, Loud Tables, and Open Doors* (Intervarsity Press, 2020). See Chapter 3, "Vibrancy," especially pages 71–76.

14. Vern L. Bengston et al., *Families and Faith*, chapter 7, "Interruptions in Religious Continuity: Rebels, Zealots, and Prodigals."

15. Psychologist Christian Smith, in his excellent book *Handing Down the Faith: How Parents Pass Their Religion on to the Next Generation*, drives the same point home: it is the lived witness of parents — not religious instruction alone — that forms the hearts of children. Your example matters more than your lectures. Smith's research leaves parents with one unavoidable conclusion: If you want to pass on the faith, the best thing you can do is become a saint. A real saint — not someone who pretends to be perfect, but someone who is visibly striving for holiness, who repents, who forgives, and who invites their children to join them on that path. To be clear, authenticity does not mean perfection. In fact, we often hear stories from men and women who say that the greatest spiritual gift their parents or grandparents ever gave them was the courage to say, "I was wrong. Please forgive me." When parents do that, they create a family culture where forgiveness is normal. They give their children a version of the faith that is resilient, real, and attainable. No one can give a sin-free witness to the Gospel. But every parent can give a humble one. And that kind of witness leaves a mark. See Christian Smith and Amy Adamczyk, *Handing Down the Faith: How Religion is Passed Across Generations* (Oxford University Press, 2021).

Chapter 6: Men for the Kingdom

1. When it comes specifically to the spiritually generative nature of priestly celibacy, I am indebted first to a conversation with Fr. Carter Griffin, and then to his excellent dissertation: Carter Griffin, "*Spiritual Fatherhood Through Priestly Celibacy*" (S.T.D. diss., Pontifical University of the Holy Cross, 2010). This scholarly work later became a superb popular book which I wholeheartedly recommend: Carter Griffin, *Why Celibacy?: Reclaiming the*

Fatherhood of the Priest (Emmaus Road, 2019).

2. For further reading on the mutual illumination of marriage and celibacy, see John Paul II, *Man and Woman He Created Them: A Theology of the Body*, 2nd ed., trans. Michael Waldstein (Pauline Books & Media, 2006), especially audiences 73–86 on virginity and celibacy lived "for the sake of the kingdom" in relation to marriage. See also Erik Varden's excellent book, *Chastity: Reconciliation of the Senses* (Bloomsbury Continuum, 2023), 102–112.

Chapter 7: Carving Pathways Forward

1. Scholars across disciplines have noted the seismic consequences of contraception and the sexual revolution on men, women, and the family. For a rigorous Catholic analysis, see Mary Eberstadt, *Adam and Eve After the Pill: Paradoxes of the Sexual Revolution* (Ignatius Press, 2013) and her follow-up volume, *Adam and Eve After the Pill, Revisited* (Ignatius Press, 2023). For a sociological study of sexual behavior in late modernity, see Mark Regnerus, *Cheap Sex: The Transformation of Men, Marriage, and Monogamy* (Oxford University Press, 2017). Finally, for a secular perspective on the weakening of male identity in a contraceptive culture, see Lionel Tiger, *The Decline of Males: The First Look at an Unexpected New World for Men and Women* (St. Martin's Press, 2000).

2. Dave Chappelle, "Sticks & Stones," directed by Stan Lathan, Netflix, 2019.

3. Data from the U.S. Census Bureau confirms that in 1960 about 9% of American children lived in single-parent households; by 2020 that figure had risen to roughly 25% (see "Living Arrangements of Children," U.S. Census Bureau, revised November 7, 2024, https://www.census.gov/data/tables/time-series/demo/families/children.html, table CH-1). For more recent analysis, see Joseph Chamie, "America's Single-Parent Households and Missing Fathers," *N-IUSSP*, January 13, 2025, https://www.niussp.org/family-and-households/americas-single-parent-households-and-missing-fathers/.

On the broader family structure question, recent data shows that just over half of high school seniors live with both of their biological parents, meaning that less than half of American children reach adulthood with their father in the home. See Nicholas Zill, "Growing Up with Mom and Dad: New Data Confirm the Tide Is Turning," *Institute for Family Studies* (blog), June 18, 2021, https://ifstudies.org/blog/growing-up-with-mom-and-dad-new-data-confirm-the-tide-is-turning.

4. Paul VI's *Humanae Vitae* (1968), paragraph 17, warned that the widespread acceptance of contraception would lead to marital infidelity, a general lowering of moral standards, the objectification of women, and coercive policies by governments. Each of these predictions has been amply borne out in the decades since. For accessible introductions and deeper study, see Christopher West, *Theology of the Body for Beginners: A Basic Introduction to St. John Paul II's Sexual Revolution*, rev. ed. (Ascension Press, 2009); Mary Eberstadt, *Adam and Eve After the Pill: Paradoxes of the Sexual Revolution*; and Mary Eberstadt, *Adam and Eve After the Pill, Revisited.* See also the numerous works of Janet E. Smith, especially her edited volume *Why Humanae Vitae Was Right: A Reader* (Ignatius Press, 1993).

5. See Leonard Sax, *Boys Adrift: The Five Factors Driving the Growing Epidemic of Unmotivated Boys and Underachieving Young Men* (Basic Books, 2009). Sax argues that a convergence of cultural, environmental, and biological factors is driving boys away from academic achievement and meaningful adult roles, leading to what he calls a "failure to launch" crisis in young men. See also David C. Geary, *Male, Female: The Evolution of Human Sex Differences* (American Psychological Association, 1998). Geary presents a biological and evolutionary account of cognitive and behavioral sex differences, showing how educational systems often fail to accommodate boys' distinct learning profiles, particularly in language and literacy. For a contemporary analysis, see Richard V. Reeves, *Of Boys and Men: Why the Modern Male Is Struggling, Why It Matters, and What to Do About It* (Brookings Institution Press, 2024). Reeves contends that boys and men are experiencing a modern identity and achievement crisis, falling behind in education, employment, and family life, largely due to structural changes in the economy, education, and gender expectations. See also *Lost Boys: State of the Nation* (The Centre for Social Justice, 2025), https://www.centreforsocialjustice.org.uk/wp-content/uploads/2025/03/CSJ-The_Lost_Boys.pdf. The report highlights systemic educational and social failures that disproportionately harm boys, particularly those from working-class backgrounds, leading to academic underperformance, behavioral issues, and reduced life opportunities.

6. I have never seen this point made as eloquently as it is made by Ray Baumeister. See Baumeister, *Is There Anything Good About Men?* In the third and fourth chapters (particularly pp. 52–60), Baumeister discusses how men have historically been tasked with dangerous, dirty, and grueling work, contributing to society's survival while suffering higher mortality and injury rates. He emphasizes that men's dominance in the workforce was often more about duty and sacrifice than privilege or control.

7. The Centre for Social Justice, *Lost Boys*. Pages 42–48 specifically address male displacement in the workforce, noting the collapse of traditional "male" jobs, the skills gap in emerging industries, and the psychological toll of economic redundancy on men.

8. Tiger, *The Decline of Males*, 67.

9. Men consistently experience a deeper level of existential and health-related distress when they are unemployed. See Mikko Laaksonen et al., "Health Consequences of Unemployment in Europe: A 13-Country Comparative Study," *International Archives of Occupational and Environmental Health* 82, no. 6 (2009): 639–49; Jenny Gulliford, "Research Indicates That Men Are More Likely to Suffer Adverse Health Consequences as a Result of Being Unemployed Than Women," *London School of Economics Politics and Policy* (blog), June 16, 2014, https://blogs.lse.ac.uk/politicsandpolicy/men-are-more-likely-to-suffer-adverse-health-consequences-as-a-result-of-unemployment-than-women/; Christopher D. Hirsch and Clay Routledge, "Existential Isolation of Males," *Psychology Today*, June 5, 2018, https://www.psychologytoday.com/us/blog/the-big-questions/201806/existential-isolation-why-is-it-higher-among-males.

10. "Young Americans Are Becoming More Religious," *The Economist*, May 4, 2025, https://www.economist.com/united-states/2025/05/04/young-americans-are-becoming-more-religious; American Enterprise Institute, "AEI Survey on Religion Among Generation Z," *American Enterprise Institute*, March 2025, https://www.aei.org/research-products/report/aei-survey-on-religion-generation-z-2025/; and Russell Contreras, "Gen Z Men Return to Church," *Axios*, May 10, 2025, https://www.axios.com/2025/05/10/religious-young-people-christianity-rise.

11. Leonard Sax, *Boys Adrift*; Michael Gurian, *The Wonder of Boys: What Parents, Mentors and Educators Can Do to Shape Boys into Exceptional Men* (Tarcher/Penguin, 1997). Both Sax and Gurian highlight the developmental differences between boys and girls, arguing that boys benefit from pedagogical and formational approaches that allow for movement, risk, and male mentorship.

12. Leonard Sax, *Why Gender Matters: What Parents and Teachers Need to Know About the Emerging Science of Sex Differences*, 2nd ed. (Harmony, 2017); Michael Gurian, *The Wonder of Men: Seventy-Six Steps to Personal and Spiritual Growth* (Tarcher/Putnam, 1999). These works emphasize that adult men, no less than boys, benefit from male-only environments where they can share vulnerabilities, form deep bonds, and pursue spiritual and personal growth in ways often less accessible in mixed company.

13. I heartily recommend Jon Tyson's book, *The Intentional Father: A Practical Guide to Raise Sons of Courage and Character* (Baker Books, 2021). Tyson provides practical exercises and spiritual frameworks for fathers seeking to actively shape their sons into mature, virtuous men. See especially pages 59–65, where he walks through the "Day Your Son Leaves Home" exercise, a visualization practice designed to help fathers clarify the goals of their parenting and craft an intentional path forward.

14. Thank you to Chris Vander Woude for assistance on the details of Tom's story. Also, please note that during the drafting of this story, formal steps have been taken to advance Tom's cause for canonization. Find out more here: www.tvwguild.org

About the Author

Dr. John Bishop is the founder and executive director of Forge, an apostolate dedicated to strengthening families through the formation of men. Founded in Des Moines in 2023, Forge is now expanding to other cities across the country. Dr. Bishop holds a doctorate in theology from The Catholic University of America and is a sought-after speaker at conferences, retreats, and seminars throughout the United States and internationally. He lives in Des Moines with his wife, Katelyn, and their children.